The Guns of
World War II

THE GUNS
OF WORLD WAR II
Ian V. Hogg

A Macdonald Illustrated War Study

MACDONALD AND JANE'S · LONDON

44031929
02194352

Contents

First published in 1976 by
Macdonald and Jane's Publishers Limited
Paulton House, 8 Shepherdess Walk
London N1 7LW

Printed in Great Britain by
REDWOOD BURN LIMITED
Trowbridge and Esher

ISBN 0 356 08246 6

INTRODUCTION

The Second World War was such a complicated and wide-ranging conflict that even now, thirty-odd years afterwards, it is still possible to find aspects of it which are relatively undocumented and unknown. One such aspect is the development and employment of artillery; with one or two notable exceptions the accounts and histories take for granted the contribution made by artillery. The guns always appeared to be there when wanted, ammunition always seemed to be supplied, the shells always landed at the right time and in the right parish, and this assessment holds good whether one looks at the British, American, German, Russian or any other nation's accounts.

This, of course, is what guns are for: to provide support when and where needed without making a fuss over it. But study of the records shows that this standard of performance was only possible because the gunners had made a good deal of fuss in peacetime, before battle was joined, ensuring that when the day came it found them with the guns, the ammunition, the communications, and the ability to weld these items into a powerful fighting arm.

The development of the artillery arms of the Second World War began before the smoke of the First had cleared away. The quantity of artillery deployed in 1914-18 astonished the soldiers; it has been estimated that in some of the major battles of 1916-17 there were more supporting gunners than attacking infantrymen, but even so there seemed to be some deficiencies, both tactical and technical, and the first post-war task was to find out what could profitably be learned for the future. The second task was to design and develop guns which would allow those lessons to be profitably applied. It is for this reason that the story has to begin in the 1920s in order that the reason behind the development decisions can be seen and understood and in order to explain how and why the artillery of the Second World War took the shape it did.

One of the most difficult aspects of rearmament is the delicate balance between finance, production and the threat of war; the gamble on being able to afford and produce new weapons in sufficient quantity to have the army fully equipped when the war begins; the Americans almost got it right, so that their new generation of artillery was beginning to flow from the production lines in 1941 when they entered the war. Britain and Russia almost got it wrong, their new weapons only beginning to flow after the war had begun, and they were both forced to begin fighting with guns a generation or more old. The Germans, in a better position to guess, failed to get it entirely right and were trying to catch up throughout the war period in some areas. Because of this the struggle to produce better weapons did not stop when the war began but increased in intensity as new threats appeared and new weapons had to be developed in order to counter them, a leap-frog progression which is best seen in the battles against bigger and stronger tanks and higher and faster aircraft.

Inevitably, there are areas of the story which lack of space precludes our exploring further, and the picture drawn here has had to be selective, dealing with aspects which are illustrative of the general development or which illustrate some specific areas of technical interest. In similar fashion, not every theatre of war has had equal treatment, examples of actions being chosen for their pertinence rather than on geographical grounds. The contribution of artillery to the war was so vast that it is impossible to be other than selective; our only hope is that the majority of the subjects discussed are of interest to the majority of readers.

Finally, I would like to acknowledge my debt to various people who have assisted me in the writing of this book: to Peter Endsleigh Castle for his excellent drawings; the Royal Artillery Institution, Woolwich for their unfailing helpfulness in making documents and books available for inspection; Commander Dave Kirchner of the US Navy for his detailed descriptions of Japanese coast defences; Mr. E.C. Bull of Ramsgate for much valued information of the wartime defences of Dover; and Dipl. Ing. Franz Kosar of Vienna for information on German artillery.

Chapter 1
REARMAMENT

Within two years of the Armistice in 1918, the armies of the western world were reduced to pale shadows of their wartime strengths as the citizen soldiers were demobilised, the wartime contracts terminated and the national finances turned to other accounts. Although the professional soldiers had few illusions, they were regarded as being tainted with the 'warmonger' image, and their attempts to insist on the retention of credible military forces were regarded with suspicion, if not with outright hostility. The Great War had been fought to end wars, so wars were ended; a League of Nations would now ensure that no war-like act could achieve its aims, since any overt hostility would be countered instantly by the united action of the League. Vast armies were no longer necessary; the only question lay in how quickly they might be decently dismantled.

With such political thinking, it took determined and far-seeing men to resist the siren's call and devote themselves to the questions of how to fight the next war, how best to employ the limited manpower and funds available, and how to improve the equipment with which to fight. Most of the military historians who have dealt with the inter-war period have concerned themselves with the faltering rise of the tank, giving the impression that this was the only piece of machinery which held any interest for the soldiers of the day. While the tank and its many problems undoubtedly did fascinate a lot of soldiers, it was not the only weapon in the armoury, and a great deal of thought was being devoted to that other great martial symbol, the gun.

The First World War had been, in many respects, an artillery war, for the simple reason that it became a gigantic siege operation, and the accepted way of conducting a siege was to bring a battering train of artillery to bear. This, in turn, invites the besieged to muster their own artillery in strength in order to seek out and destroy the battering train, and the troops attempting to assault the breaches made by the guns. As a result, more and bigger guns were demanded in order to deliver greater quantities of shells on to the other side, and the resulting advances in artillery technology during the years 1914-18 were considerable. It might be assumed from this that by 1920 the artilleries of the world were provided with ample quantities of the latest designs of weapons and were unlikely to demand anything fresh for many years ahead, and, generally speaking, this was the attitude taken by their various financial masters. But the technical truth was less reassuring; during the Second World War a British expert observed that gun development was akin to a savings bank. One paid in, in basic research, during peacetime, and one drew out, in weapon design and production, in war. On this assessment, the world's artillery was approaching insolvency; the rapid expansion of the war years had used up all the prewar store of research information. It was time to get back to fundamentals. Moreover, except for a few wartime designs (most of which were admitted to be defective in one respect or another) the guns which saw the close of the war were little more than improved models of those which were either in service or on the drawing board at the war's beginning, and every available ounce of improvement had been wrung from them. Further improvement to give more range, more velocity or whatever was needed, would necessitate fresh designs.

And further improvement was demanded by gunners, even though they appreciated the problems, financial, political and technical, which faced them. The war had scarcely finished when earnest committees were examining the performance of artillery, analysing results, studying war reports and accounts of battles in order to determine what lessons could be learned and how best they could be applied. It was this analysis, and the recommendations and opinions of these bodies which, in the long term, determined the equipment, tactics and operation of artillery during the Second World War.

In Britain the principal lessons were held to be, firstly, the enormous weight of artillery fire needed to support an attack against a defended position if the attack was to have any hope of success. The second, stemming from this, was that the command structure must be centralised so that large numbers of guns could be rapidly brought under one hand for a particular operation; yet the same structure had to be sufficiently flexible to be able to accommodate different natures and numbers of guns on different occasions, and also be able to de-centralise control for operations demanding rapid and independent movement. Thirdly, a system of planning fire support had to be perfected in order to give maximum support to the attacking infantry, produce it quickly, and yet still be capable of reverting to a defensive role at a moment's notice. Fourthly, a decision had to be made between the relative importance of surprise and destruction. Many attacks during the war had been preceded by massive artillery bombardments, often lasting for days, which effectively destroyed enemy installations, but at the same time advertised the forthcoming attack and, as a by-product, so thoroughly wrecked the landscape as to make it well-nigh impassable for the assaulting troops. On the other hand, attacks in which a short and sudden bombardment had taken the enemy by surprise had frequently succeeded, in spite of doing less material damage. This knotty problem of balance had to be argued out at great length.

Fifthly came the question of communication. Time and time again, artillery support had failed at an advanced stage of an attack due to the difficulty which observers accompanying the infantry had in communicating with the guns in order to call for fire support, modify planned support or indicate fresh targets.

Lastly came the demand for more range from the guns; this was a product of frequent experience where advancing troops had outrun the available range of field artillery, largely because the artillery had to be sited some five to six thousand yards behind the front line in order to secure it from mortar attack or sudden raids and allow it sufficient time in case of an enemy attack to be able to retaliate before the enemy reached the gun position. And with field guns having a maximum range of about 9,000 yards, this didn't leave much advance before the troops were out of the gun's range. Needless to say, this demand for extra range was never left unaccompanied by other technical demands. An example of the approach can be seen in this extract from an entry for a military essay competition in the late 1920s: 'An artillery weapon must permit of accuracy, combined with rapidity of fire, long range, wide traverse, speed in and out of action, and adequate weight of shell for the task in hand.'

One can hardly argue with that assessment in terms of desirability, but as a practical engineering proposition it is a mass of contradictions, and one of the first questions in front of the analysts was the one of how best to balance these conflicting and varying requests. Major (Brevet Lt Col) A. H. Brooke, RA (later to become Field Marshal Lord Alanbrooke) summed up the dilemma in the concluding paragraph of a series of articles on the 'Evolution of Artillery in the Great War' published in the 'Journal of the Royal Artillery' in 1929:

'Periods of peace produce a tendency to increase mobility at the expense of fire power, whilst war has always demonstrated that mobility is dependent upon fire power in the field of battle . . . We are . . . faced with the grave danger of sacrificing fire power to mobility. If we can avoid this end, we shall have learned to apply the primary lesson of the Great War.'

The whole question of mobility and power came down to a very basic consideration — how the gun was to be taken into battle. The normal fashion was to tow it behind a team of six horses, and this automatically imposed an upper limit on weight. After allowing for the weight of the ammunition limber, the British standard for a field gun was thirty hundredweight (3,360lb), while the Americans laid down 4,500lb. But the arrival of the petrol engine had shown that this need no longer apply so stringently. As early as May 1919 the American Army's 'Caliber Board' reported that 'we have developed the use of man and animal power practically to the limit. The use of good roads and railroads is well understood, but now we are in a way to conquer the broadest field, that is cross-country, by the use of mechanical transport.' The British Director of Artillery in January 1922, in a discussion of a suitable weapon for Horse Artillery, observed, 'it is desired to consider the use of existing equipments, i.e. the 18-pounder or 4.5-inch howitzer, to be drawn by a tractor.'

While artillerymen in general were devotees of the horse — and many still are — they were a good deal less reactionary about the advent of motorisation than were the cavalry. This was probably due to their greater experience during the war of trying to maintain horses in a fit condition under appalling conditions of service. Their only reservation was in the matter of reliability. One shell splinter, they argued, might kill one horse in a team, whereupon the remaining five could still pull the gun; but the same splinter could immobilise a tractor and with it the gun. Mechanical reliability was also at an early stage, though it was accepted that this might well improve with time. As a result of all this the weight limitation on guns was, for the purpose of planning and research at least, relaxed. An interesting comment appears in a Royal Artillery Committee Minute for 1925, on the subject of a proposed new design of field howitzer:

'The Committee would be glad to be informed whether 30cwt is considered to be the absolute maximum weight of this equipment. Whatever is decided, the new equipment will not materialise for some years, and by that time, presumably, mechanical transport will have made further headway.'

Allowing that mobility might well be improved, the next question was the power of the gun, an amalgam of maximum range and weight of

The 18-pounder Mark 4, the 1918 version which showed considerable improvement on the original 1904 model. With pneumatic tyres and a new design of split trail, it was to serve until the 1940s and, with a new 3.45-inch barrel, became the 18/25-pounder.

The 77mm Feld-kanone 16, the back-bone of Germany's wartime field artillery. Later fitted with a 75mm barrel it was to continue in service during the Second World War in small numbers.

shell. Obviously a small-calibre gun could, with a sufficiently powerful cartridge, send a shell a long way, but the effect on the enemy would be minimal. Conversely, a heavy and effective shell invariably meant less range and, with it, a heavier weapon to withstand the shock of firing. The standard British field gun of the time was the 18-pounder (3.30-inch calibre) which had been developed in 1904 and, in a succession of improved models, had proved to be the backbone of the Royal Artillery in France and the best field gun to emerge from the war. This latter claim was, of course, hotly disputed by the French and Americans who championed the French 75mm Model 1897, the archetypal 'quick-firing gun', but the facts were beyond dispute by 1919: the 18-pounder fired an 18lb shell to 9,300 yards, while the 75mm fired a 12lb shell to 7,500 yards. The German equivalent had been a 77mm firing a 16lb shell to 9,900 yards, an interesting intermediate point.

The other weapon used in direct support of the infantry was the light field howitzer and here again, Britain, with a 1904 model 4.5-inch firing a 35lb shell to 7,300 yards was well provided. The French had no equivalent weapon (their army had lobbied persistently for one for many years and had been refused finance to develop one), while the German Army used a 1916 model 105mm calibre firing a 34lb shell to 9,100 yards.

Comparison of those weapons and their wartime performance led to wide discussion over what was the best form to adopt; a gun, with relatively high velocity, fixed charge, flat trajectory, light shell and long range? Or a howitzer, of less range but with a heavier shell, multiple charges to give a variety of trajectories, and relatively low velocity? The ideal, of course, was to have as many of both as you needed, so that whatever the task, there was the right weapon to suit; this was the policy of perfection recommended by the Caliber Board when they reported:

'The consensus of opinion of artillery officers is that the division artillery missions are best fulfilled by a light field gun and a light howitzer having a range of at least 11,000 yards.'

And they went on to recommend the development of a 75mm gun with a range of 15,000 yards and a 105mm howitzer with a range of 12,000 yards.

In Britain the recommendation stage did not come until later in the 1920s, by which time the 'Ten Year Rule' was in force, the Geddes Axe had fallen, and it was obvious that whatever was decided on would take a long time to reach production. As a result there were a wide variety of possible solutions to every class of gun being canvassed. The private gunmakers, Vickers, Beardmore, the Elswick Ordnance Company, the Coventry Ordnance Works, and the official design establishments were, from time to time, given sets of figures and asked to produce a likely solution on paper. These were examined and, if one idea sounded reasonable, a wooden mock-up would be commissioned so that some idea of the utility of the finished article could be gained. A drill could be evolved, gunners could be clustered around it to 'go through the motions' and thus discover defects in the design which rarely made themselves apparent on paper plans, and various conclusions could be drawn. Then it was back to the Committee Room to draw up a fresh specification and start again. During the 1920s the Royal Artillery Committee investigated — very thoroughly — over twenty gun designs. These included an 18-pounder howitzer and a 20-pounder gun for Horse

Wooden mock-up of a potential Horse Artillery gun, developed in Wool-wich Arsenal in the 1920s. Such models gave the assessment committees some idea of what a paper design might look like and whether it could be conveniently handled.

A prototype Vickers 105mm gun demonstrating its 'articulation' or ability to be put into action on uneven ground and remain stable.

Artillery; a 3-inch pack artillery gun; a 3-inch 41-calibre (i.e. the barrel was 41 calibres – 41 x 3 inches – long) gun, a 3.9-inch howitzer and a 4.13-inch howitzer, all for field artillery; three different designs of self-propelled 18-pounder gun (two of which actually entered service, though in scant numbers); 4.5-inch, 5-inch and 6-inch medium guns and a 6-inch medium howitzer; 8-inch, 8.8-inch and 9.2-inch heavy howitzers; 3.3-inch, 3.6-inch, 3.7-inch and 4.7-inch anti-aircraft guns on wheeled, tracked and self-propelled mountings; 6-pounder twin and 15-inch coastal guns (principally with Singapore in mind); and even a light

The Birch Gun, an 18-pounder mounted on to a modified Vickers tank chassis. Notice the complicated fuze setters and sighting apparatus on the gun mounting.

The Birch Gun in the anti-aircraft role. It was this requirement which led to the profusion of sights and fuze setters, duplicating those needed for ground fire.

3-pounder proposed as an infantry-accompanying gun. All these were the subject of careful paper studies; most of them reached the mock-up stage; some were actually built in prototype form and fired. But of that entire list, only three – the two coast guns and the 3.7-inch anti-aircraft gun – ever managed to survive the course and reach service, the few 18-pounder self-propelled guns having been cast aside by 1930.

An equally impressive list could be drawn up of American experimental equipments of the same period, and one with much the same sort of final result. But at least all this work, generally performed by a handful of men backed up by relatively small technical facilities and a derisory sum of money, served to eliminate the worst ideas and concentrate design effort on the more feasible solutions. And in both Britain and America it slowly became apparent that finance and manufacturing facilities were never going to permit the luxury of both a field gun and a field howitzer, and so a decision had better be made. In both cases, the decision was the same: a gun-howitzer, a cross-breed at which both establishments shuddered when the idea was first mooted, but one which, reluctantly, both saw to be the only possible answer.

The gun-howitzer attempts – with some degree of success, let it be admitted – to marry the better points of both types of weapon into one equipment. The principal key to this is the design of the ammunition; in 1918 it was an accepted fact that a gun used a round of fixed ammunition, that is, a round in which shell and cartridge case were firmly fixed together, the case containing the propelling charge. It follows from this that the propelling charge could not be adjusted, and for any range the

gun could have but one trajectory. A disadvantage which went with this system was that since the *raison d'être* of the gun was range, the charge was as powerful as the gun would stand, and thus the rate at which the gun wore out was at a maximum. Much of the gun's shooting was, in fact, at lesser ranges than the maximum, ranges where the powerful charge, with its attendent high velocity and wear, were not needed; but the fixed round ensured that they were always there. Eventually, during

American gunners at practice with the 155mm M1918 howitzer in the 1930s. The howitzer was of French origin and adopted by the USA during 1917-18. Up-dated by pneumatic tyres it served well into the Second World War.

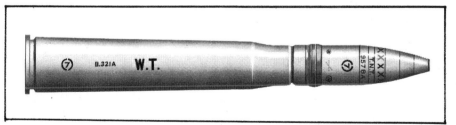

the war, most guns were provided with alternative rounds having reduced charges; these could be used for the short-range work and thus cut down the rate of wear. But that was an awkward solution.

A fixed round of ammunition in which cartridge and shell form one unit. Desirable in cases where rapid fire is needed — as in anti-tank or anti-aircraft guns — but it becomes awkward and heavy in large calibres.

The howitzer, on the other hand, used a separate round, the shell and cartridge being two separate components. The propelling charge was divided into a number of individual sections, any of which could be removed or combined to vary the power of the charge, giving the howitzer as many different trajectories as it had charges for much of its range. This system had the additional virtue that the charge selected

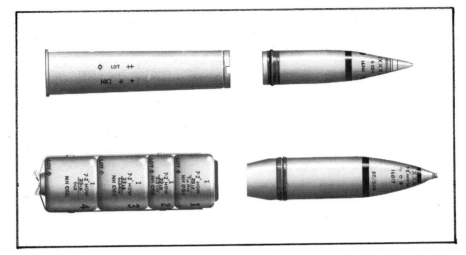

A separate-loading round in which the cartridge case and projectile are separate units and are loaded separately. In this example the cartridge is inside a brass case, the propellant being packed in cloth bags so that the charge can be adjusted to give the desired ballistics.

A separate-loading round for a bagged-charge gun; the charge is in cloth bags and can be separated into smaller units if required. The gun breech has to be sealed to prevent gas leakage, a job performed by the brass case on guns using cased cartridges.

need be no more powerful than was necessary to get the shell to the desired range, which led to the reduction of wear and a longer useful life. The howitzer shell would be heavier than that used in a gun of the same calibre, it would be fired at a lower velocity, and the low velocity would lead to high trajectories which could pass over intervening terrain features and drop the shell into otherwise inaccessible places.

In order to reach a compromise, the gun-howitzer uses a barrel longer than that usual with a howitzer though shorter than that of a gun; it fires a shell of median weight; and it uses an adjustable propelling charge whose maximum is such as to produce a high velocity and give the weapon gun-like performance, but the lower charges of which reduce the velocity and give the weapon the flexibility of a howitzer. The ammunition needs to be separable so as to be able to adjust the charge, which means either using separate ammunition as described above – the German and British solution – or, another compromise, the 'semi-fixed' round adopted by the Americans, a round which comes in one piece, can be separated for charge adjustment, and then re-connected to form a one-piece unit for loading.

The British Army were drawn to the gun-howitzer some time in the late 1920s after reviewing a variety of guns and howitzers and thrashing out exactly what the future field artillery weapon was to be expected to do. The basic demand was always the same – whatever came or went from the specification, the weapon had to be able to shoot to 15,000 yards, a demand which appears to have first been stated officially in 1924 but one which, eventually, had to be watered down. In 1925 the Ordnance Committee were asked to consider a 105mm howitzer which would range to 12,000 yards with a 33lb shell, and in 1926 this proposal was elaborated into a set of 'General Conditions' to guide contractors. This specified mechanical traction, solid-tyred wheels and a 35lb shell, among other things. Later in 1926 the Commandant of the School of Artillery made some observations about the problem of shooting at

The prototype Vickers 4.1-inch howitzer of 1930. A breech-loading bag charge gun, it was not accepted in this form but the carriage design (except for the wheels) was perpetuated in the 25-pounder.

moving tanks, indicating some mechanical features of the current 18-pounder which were objectionable in this role, and giving some suggestions for future weapon design.

After considering these and other comments, in January 1927 a decision was reached as to the main requirements of the new gun: it had to range to 12,000 yards – though the possibility of reaching the magic 15,000 yards with a 'super-charge' cartridge and a special shell were not to be lost sight of; the weight had not to be more than 30cwt in action; it had to have sighting and carriage features designed with anti-tank shooting in mind; and it was to be designed for mechanical traction with a maximum speed of 12 mph on the road.

This proposal was considered throughout the year and various opinions taken, and in January 1928 a specification appeared which re-iterated the basic proposals and added that the calibre was to be 3.3 inches, the shell was to weigh 18½lb, and the round would be a fixed round, though three alternative loadings, super-charge, normal charge and reduced charge, were to be available. This eminently reasonable specification was then completed by the demand that it should be possible to elevate the gun to 45° in order that it should perform as an anti-aircraft gun, and suitable sights for this application were to be provided. This dual role, field and anti-aircraft, was a feature which had been lusted after ever since 1915; in the earliest days when aircraft were low and slow, there was some faint air of utility about it, but by the late 1920's it should have been obvious that only a specialist weapon could hope to compete in the vertical role, and the retention of this dual-purpose demand for such a long time indicates a blind spot in professional thinking. It should be said that the United States Army pursued this idea long after the British had reluctantly given it up as impractical; a dual-purpose 75mm 'divisional gun' which could function in both roles was being toyed with as late as 1938.

This specification was examined for a long time, until in January 1929 the ballistic experts pointed out that the demand was excessive, since the chamber pressure necessary inside the gun to obtain the desired performance was going to be a good deal higher than predicted by the gun designers. The only solution would be to re-design the gun to a higher factor of safety, which would have meant an increase in weight.

During the next three years or so this 3.3-inch gun, plus a 3.7-inch and a 3-inch were discussed and analysed from every possible angle. At the same time Vickers built a prototype 4.1-inch (105mm) howitzer which was test-fired. After more discussion, in October 1933 a 3.45-inch gun-howitzer firing a 25lb shell was proposed, and in December of that year the question of it becoming the universal field artillery weapon was broached. Finally, in September 1934, the Director Royal Artillery ordered the construction of a pilot model of the 'Universal Field Artillery Weapon' and the 25-pounder gun-howitzer was finally launched.

In a similar fashion the United States Artillery had gradually swung from the Caliber Board's recommendation for two weapons to acceptance of the gun-howitzer solution in 105mm calibre – though they always spoke of it as a howitzer and refused to acknowledge the existence of such an expression as 'gun-howitzer'. Their adoption of this design came back to the same root causes as the British adoption of the 25-pounder, the need for adequate shell power on the target, since the criterion of what was adequate had been drastically revised as a result of experience in 1914-18.

In 1914 the standard field gun projectile was the shrapnel shell; the British 18-pounder, for example, carried 375 lead/antimony balls, the French 75mm 300. By using a time fuze the shell was exploded in the air, short of the target, discharging the balls forward and downward at a velocity slightly greater than the remaining velocity of the shell. Against unprotected troops in the open, which was the standard target in 1914, the result was murderous and, indeed, against such a target shrapnel could hardly be surpassed even today. But once soldiers began to dig, and once they had overhead cover, the shrapnel shell was useless. It was also useless against any sort of obstacle – wire, field-works, pillboxes, tanks – all the impedimenta of the battlefield which the First World War produced. As a result, the high explosive shell, which prior to 1914 had been the prerogative of the howitzer, was in demand for field guns. This, in fact, was the root of the 'Shell Scandal' which Lloyd George manipulated so advantageously in 1915; the shortage was less of shells as such than of high explosive shells, which were being demanded for field guns at a rate never imagined nor anticipated. The 1920s reverberated with the arguments over shrapnel versus high explosive but the facts

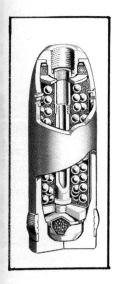

Shrapnel shell, showing the arrangement of bullets around the central flash channel and the gunpowder expelling charge behind.

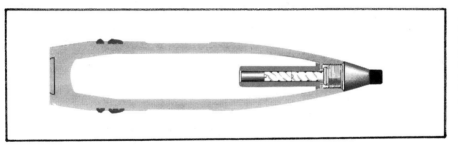

A high-explosive shell, illustrating its relative simplicity compared with shrapnel. The central channel carries a charge of more sensitive explosive to transfer the detonation from the fuze to the main explosive filling.

were plain enough that if warfare remained in the same pattern, the shrapnel shell was finished as a worthwhile artillery projectile.

On the other hand the high explosive shell was far from being a satisfactory replacement. The wartime shells, hurriedly designed, used a thick-walled shell in order to utilize low-grade steel and retain the necessary strength to withstand being fired from the gun. As a result the explosive content was low; an 18-pounder shell had only 13 ounces of high explosive inside it, a useful payload of only $4\frac{1}{2}$ per cent of the total weight. Because of this low content and poor steel, the fragments into which the shell split upon detonation were much larger than the optimum desirable for producing casualties and they were moving at too low a velocity to travel far from the point of burst.

What followed from this was a two-fold argument: firstly the shell had to be improved so as to carry more explosive, break up into smaller fragments and distribute them at higher velocity; and secondly to look for the largest calibre of field gun which would allow a useful size of shell to be fired and yet stay within acceptable weight and size limits. It was this latter consideration which steered the British and Americans away from the gun and led to the adoption of the gun-howitzer, a step up in calibre to allow a more effective shell to be produced.

We have looked in some detail at the gestation of the field artillery weapons, since they exemplify the sort of arguments and compromises which were going on in every artillery area. Next in importance to the field gun in the 1920s was the anti-aircraft gun, and similar tales could be told of the gradual fining-down processes which led to the eventual choices, did space allow. Suffice it to say that by the early 1930s the United States had decided to develop three guns: a 90mm mobile equipment for field army use, a 105mm for static emplacement, and a mobile 4.7-inch for rear area employment. Britain decided to retain the 3-inch gun which had served throughout the First World War, and after trials with a very advanced design of 3.6-inch gun in the early 1920s decided, in October 1928, to develop a 4.7-inch static gun and a 3.7-inch mobile model.

In the matter of heavy artillery a new element had entered the argument: the aeroplane. As early as 1919 a paper in the 'Journal of the Royal Artillery' (Vol XLVI, No. 3, p129) by Lt Col R. G. Cherry, MC, RAF, entitled 'The Aeroplane as a Long Range Gun', spelled out the

The 3.6-inch A A
Gun developed
between 1918 and
1926. The tracked
carriage was towed
by the traction
engine in the back-
ground. Notice that
four men can be seen
attending to the
sighting while two
load the gun.

The 12-inch
howitzer in posi-
tion. The traction
engine wheels of the
transport waggons
can be seen behind,
and the steel box
under the muzzle
had to be filled with
earth to keep the
weapon stable when
it fired.

view of the infant Royal Air Force. Its closing line was '. . . it looks as if
the areoplane bomb will almost entirely supersede the shell thrown
heretofore with such accuracy by the guns of the Royal Regiment.' Lt
Col Cherry was followed by many more persuasive arguers, and the
arguments appeared to be clinched when the question of moving heavy
guns at the anticipated speed of armoured formations came to be con-

sidered. The 9.2-inch howitzer was a 16-ton monster which had to be anchored in place by a steel box filled with 11 tons of soil, and it moved in three loads behind heavy and ponderous tractors. The 12-inch was even more cumbersome; 37 tons of gun, 20 tons of earth to be shovelled, six wagon loads drawn by traction engines at 3 mph; it was no wonder the rest of the Army called it 'The Twelve-Inch Road Hog'. (Much as in later years the cumbersome anti-aircraft Radar No. 4 received the sobriquet of 'The Divisional Mobile Road-Block'.)

The Royal Air Force, anxious to find its place in the sun, assured all and sundry that improvements in aircraft, navigation, engines and bombs would rapidly put them in the position of being able to do anything the gun could do, and at a longer range into the bargain. It had to be admitted that the introduction of aircraft into the tribal wars in India and Afghanistan seemed to support this contention. The Americans too were lulled by the same song, and although designs of heavy guns were discussed from time to time there was little urgency about them and, thankfully one is inclined to think, the energy and finance available were devoted to other aspects of artillery.

If the weapons were a source of discussion, this was nothing compared to the arguments about how to use them to best effect. In the first place the 1914-18 experience had shown that previous ideas on the amount of artillery needed in an army were sadly deficient. Divisional artillery in 1914 was at the strength of six guns for every thousand rifles to be supported; by 1918 it was 13 guns per 1,000 rifles, and no reduction from that figure was considered feasible or wise. Next came the question of command: in 1914 the individual artillery batteries supported their adjacent infantry without reference to what was going on elsewhere. By 1918 the artillery was interlocked under command at Corps or even Army level, ensuring that artillery support was continuous across the front and sufficiently flexible to allow fire to be brought to bear from adjacent batteries when extra power was needed. As a result of this the wartime policy became the post-war doctrine: command of artillery was always to be at as high a level as possible. But to go with this there was to be a capability for decentralization such as would allow the homogeneous mass of defensive artillery to be split into its sub-units when the time came to engage in mobile warfare.

The next vital point was the recognition that efficient gunnery had to have a lot of technical ancillaries in order to make it work. Primary among these ancillaries was the need for fool-proof communication linking the whole of the divisional or corps or army artillery. It was little use for a forward observer with an infantry company to find a battalion of enemy sleeping in the sunshine if he couldn't communicate with sufficient guns to bring down fire upon them.

The war had brought new aids to gunnery; study of the effects of meteorological conditions upon the flight of the shell had reached the point where it was possible to make calculations of the effect of wind, air density, air temperature and similar phenomena, apply them to a map-deduced range and bearing to the target, apply the resulting information to the gun sights, fire, and land the shell within lethal distance of the target without the need for trial shots, thus obtaining the utmost surprise in an attack. This demanded a meteorological service, but since the Royal Air Force already owned one, they agreed to furnish the Royal Artillery with the necessary information; this gave the RAF another reason for justifying their existence at a time when there was no shortage of people trying to whittle it down, and it also relieved the artillery of a manpower problem.

To take advantage of the meteorological information it was axiomatic that you had to know, with some precision, exactly where your gun was and where the target was – and both locations had to be on a mutual frame of reference, so that the range and bearing between the two could be calculated. Locating the gun became an extension of the normal survey network set up by the Royal Engineers, and artillery surveyors, starting at points surveyed in by the RE, carried their survey forward to fix the guns and then further forward to fix special observation posts overlooking enemy territory. From these posts observers with instruments watched for tell-tale flashes from enemy guns, laid their instruments on them, and, by cross-observation from a number of posts, could deduce locations for enemy batteries in terms of their own survey network.

Another wartime innovation was the planting of microphones across the front, linked with a recording instrument at the rear. An observer, hearing the report of an enemy gun firing, pressed a switch activating the circuits. As the sound of the shot reached the microphones in turn, so the recorder traced a record which, with the aid of a plotting board, could be translated into a target location – again, in sympathy with the survey network.

Although these services existed by 1918, both flash-spotting and sound-ranging were originally built up in a period of static warfare when communication was relatively simple and the maintenance of miles of wire no great problem. In a similar way, the survey operation was fairly simple and not particularly fast-moving. But the promise (or premise) of mobile warfare meant that all the technical expertise had to be pared down to a transportable form and its application tailored to a war of movement. For with the range of the guns lengthening, if the targets could not be found, they could not be engaged.

One of the more unusual proposals to appear in the 1920s was that of providing the Royal Artillery with their own aircraft in order to improve their visual command of the front and enable them to bring more effective fire to bear. This had been done during the war by RAF pilots, many of whom had transferred from the artillery and thus had some knowledge and experience of gunnery. The procedure, however, was cumbersome (another case for the improvement of communications) and, since the aircraft were not under the direct control of the gunners, they were not always available when they were most needed.

But persuasive as the arguments were, the RAF would have none of it: one of the voices urging the innovation was that same Lt Col Cherry, now writing papers in the RA Journal and the 'Journal of the United Services Institute of India' (Vol LV No. 241, p33). His rashness brought a rapid reply (RA Journal Vol LIII p280) from an up-and-coming airman, Sqn Ldr J. C. Slessor, MC, RAF:

'... it is a point of view widely held and at the bottom is based on a fallacy, namely that it is possible to make reliable deductions in the air. *It is not only impossible but it is excessively dangerous.*' (Slessor's italics)

It was to be 1934 before the argument was raised again, and 1942 before it was actually settled.

If the question of finding and engaging targets was giving problems to the field gunners, it was giving even more to the anti-aircraft specialists. During the 1920s and 1930s the bomber threat assumed proportions which would have strained credulity but for the fact that the aircraft protagonists were vying with each other in their promises of performance for the next generation of aircraft. Trenchard's strategic bombing campaign of 1919 had captured many imaginations and, extrapolating from Trenchard's assumptions, the general belief

Japanese troops in China operating a 75mm anti-aircraft gun, the standard Japanese Army model which was to be hopelessly out-classed in a few years time.

throughout Europe was that a future war would commence with an all-out aerial bombardment, high explosive and poison gas bombs falling like rain on the unprotected cities beneath. One of the by-products of this dogma was that the lion's share of the pitiful sums of money allotted to the armies went towards anti-aircraft research and development; but, since even this share was derisory, little got done. In 1928 the British Army took the decision to develop a 3.7-inch gun firing a 28lb shell to a ceiling of 28,000 feet, which was the genesis of a notable weapon, but provision of guns was only part of the story.

The precise figures are in some doubt, due largely to suspiciously partisan methods of calculation, but the experience of the First World War tended to show that the guns would have to fire something like 1,800 to 2,000 shells into the air for every aircraft brought down. Admittedly, to bring the aircraft down was the ideal; it was almost as effective, from the defensive point of view, if the aircraft were forced up to an altitude from which it could not bomb with accuracy or was forced into taking some evasive action which prevented it from bombing at all. Nevertheless, 'birds downed' was the lay criterion of effectiveness and the sort of figure which critics loved to brandish; it was therefore necessary to back up the guns with a system of control which would help to bring the 'rounds per bird' figure down.

In a nutshell, the gunners' problems were these: firstly they had to detect the approach of the aircraft; secondly they had to bring aeroplane and shell into the same place at the same time; and thirdly they had to make sure the shell burst effectively when it got there. Detection relied

The German 75mm anti-aircraft gun L/60. Originally developed for export trade, a number were clandestinely supplied to the Army to form the nucleus of the Flak-artillerie.

on sensing the approach of the aircraft, and the only apparent solution to this was to detect the noise of the engines. A variety of sound detectors were produced, culminating in the massive static 'sound mirrors', parabolic concrete walls several hundred feet long constructed in the marshes alongside the Thames estuary. By concentrating the reflected sound into microphones it was possible to detect an aircraft some ten or twelve miles away – providing it was obliging enough to fly on the optimum course for the configuration of the sound mirror. At the speeds of which aircraft had been capable in 1918 – about 100 mph for a laden bomber at 10,000 feet – this would have given the guns some five or six minutes' warning. But by 1925 the aircraft were getting better; 'Textbook of Anti-Aircraft Gunnery, Volume 1' issued in that year said 'An estimate secured from the Air Force, through the Air Inventions Committee, makes it probable that within ten years 160 mph may be obtained at 10,000 feet . . .', and, adding the possible effects of upper-air winds, it concluded that 'anti-aircraft has at present the problem of dealing with machines averaging 110 or 120 mph, but varying in the neighbourhood of 40 mph on the one hand and 200 mph on the other . . .' This cut the warning to a scant three minutes.

Assuming the guns to have been warned, the next problem was to detect the target visually, measure its height, range and bearing, and engage it with fire. The principal question here lay in what the aircraft would do between the instant the shell left the gun and the instant it arrived at the same height as the aircraft. This 'time of flight' could be as much as 35 seconds, and an aircraft flying at 200 mph could travel almost two miles in that time. Hence aiming the gun directly at the aircraft when the gun was fired meant putting the shell up two miles behind it; obviously, the gun had to be aimed ahead, and it was the determination of how much to lay ahead that was at the heart of the matter. Until about 1926 it was still considered feasible to develop gun sights with various scales and deflection devices such that deflections dependent upon the aircraft's estimated height and speed could be set in so as to displace the point of aim of the sight. Pointing the displaced sight at the target would then automatically point the gun barrel at the 'future target position'. But such sights began to increase in complexity as more and more factors began to be appreciated and taken into account; as a result the 3.6 inch gun of the early 1920s had no less than five highly-skilled men setting sights and pointing the gun while two more actually loaded and fired it. The tail had begun to wag the dog, and manning the air defences with this sort of equipment was going to demand large numbers of expensively trained men.

The Americans appear to have been the first to realise the difficulties inherent in this system, and by 1923 they had abandoned the idea of aiming the gun from the gun. Instead, they adopted a system which had been in use for many years in coast defence artillery – probably because anti-aircraft defence had, by some inscrutable decision, become a coast artillery responsibility in the U.S. Army, and thus the gunners took a number of preconceived ideas with them. In coast gunnery the gun can be aimed at the target by any one of three methods or 'cases': 'Case I', in which direction and elevation were both derived from the gun sights – in other words, the normally-accepted method of aiming any weapon, such as a rifle or pistol. 'Case II', where direction was derived from the gun sight – as by a telescope pointing at the target – but elevation was applied by scale, using data supplied from some form of command post or fire control centre. 'Case III' was where the gun was aimed entirely by transmitted information, scales on the mounting being used to set the gun for both direction and elevation, and the gunners having neither the need nor in many cases the means to see the target. Using Case III the gunlayers – the men responsible for pointing the gun accurately at the target – merely had to move the gun in bearing and elevation until pointers, operated by the gun's movement, in a dial in front of the operators, lined up with pointers already set at the desired data by electrical transmission from the control post; the highly trained and high-priced specialists could now be concentrated in one place and the results of their labours passed to any number of guns.

A further saving in specialists could be made if machinery could be called in to do the routine arithmetic, and a variety of machines were now developed into which information on such things as the target's speed, height and direction, air temperature, air density, wind speed and direction, shell drift, cartridge temperature, rotation of the earth and so forth could be set and the future position of the target, defined in terms of gun data required to hit it, would emerge. In view of their function, these devices were called 'predictors'; they were almost entirely mechanical, though some models did use electricity for some of the calculations, varying voltages representing varying quantities of, for example, wind speed.

The next step was to transmit this information from the predictor to the gun, also by using electricity, and display it there in an intelligible form, and this was relatively easy. The final step, which the Americans were trying as early as 1927, was to provide the gun with power for elevating and training and then control the application of this power by the predictor output, so that there was no longer any need for a gunlayer at all; the gun would be pointed automatically by the information transmitted from the predictor, and the only men near the gun would be those concerned with loading and firing it. This was achieved by 1930, when a 3-inch remote-controlled gun was demonstrated at Aberdeen Proving Ground, but although the device worked, it was little more than a laboratory demonstration at that stage. The 'Remote Control System T1' gave an average error of two minutes of arc in elevation and nine minutes of arc in bearing, which, although not good enough for service, were remarkably good figures for a first attempt; but the system required several years of perfecting before it was accurate and reliable enough to become a service equipment.

In many ways the discovery of radar was the salvation of anti-aircraft gunnery; not only did it suddenly solve the problem of locating the target in ample time and with much greater accuracy, it also provided an all-weather, day and night, range and height finding capability which optics could never do. Moreover the intensive research into electronics which radar set in motion was to provide vastly better predictors, more reliable and precise systems of data transmission and remote control, and also, eventually, solve the problem of bursting the shell close enough to the target to guarantee lethal effect.

So far we have considered activity in Britain and the United States. But of course there were gun designers and artillery planners at work in other countries as well. And for the purpose of our narrative, we must now look at what was happening in Germany.

The Versailles Treaty had restricted Germany to an army 100,000 strong, no air force, no anti-aircraft artillery except that in the Navy and in the Fortress of Konigsberg, and no heavy artillery. The gunmaking companies were also restricted in both the size and nature of their products. But von Seekt, the head of the new Reichswehr, was one of the greatest military planners of all time, and he set to work to turn this army into an élite corps on to which a conscript army could rapidly be grafted when the time came. And although he was barred from adopting modern armament, there was no way for the Allied Disarmament Commissions to stop a concealed design office from working on paper, and von Seekt laid down a sound policy; firstly to decide what types of weapons were wanted, then to design them and from time to time make any necessary modifications to the design to keep them up to date, and at the same time to plan and make all the necessary arrangements to begin mass production at a moment's notice. The belief that the Wehrmacht sprang fully armed from one of Adolf Hitler's footprints in 1934 is not entirely correct; the mass production may have begun then, but the planning and preparation had been ten years in the making.

An example of the subterfuge which went on is the history of the German anti-aircraft artillery; the only weapons left by the Versailles Treaty were those of the sea-going Navy and a handful of guns in the Konigsberg Fortress. Everything else had to be dismantled, so the Army converted numbers of anti-aircraft guns into 'field guns' by removing the special sights and putting blocks on the elevating gear so as to limit the maximum elevation of the guns. These 'field guns' were then used to arm seven motorised 'field batteries', one of which was attached to each of the seven artillery regiments allowed to the Army under the terms of the Treaty. The officers of these batteries were then seconded to duties with the Navy, where they became anti-aircraft officers attached to warships and were duly trained in anti-aircraft gunnery techniques. In 1928 a number of 75mm anti-aircraft guns, ostensibly built commercially for export, were surreptitiously acquired by means of dummy companies, faked export orders and similar stratagems which have never been completely unravelled, and these were issued to the seven batteries to replace their 'field guns'. Fire control equipment was also provided, and the batteries were moved to remote parts of East Prussia for clandestine training in their new role.

In 1932, more batteries, without guns, were formed under the title of 'Transport Abteilungen', and shortly afterwards anti-aircraft machine gun companies were formed under the cover of the 'Deutsche Luftsport Verband'. By the time the Luftwaffe (who were responsible for anti-aircraft defence) was officially unveiled on 1 April 1935, it had its anti-aircraft department fully organised; all that was needed was a paper transaction to bring the various subterfuge organisations back under Luftwaffe control, followed by an injection of men and weapons to bring them up to strength.

In the matter of weapon development the German Army began with some considerable advantages. In the first place there was no vast store of First World War equipment standing idle, as was the case with the victors, and this meant, in turn, that they were not restrained by economic considerations to a policy of using up the obsolescent designs. There was also the powerful latent military spirit of the country; in contrast to the democracies, no right-thinking German would ever argue that money spent on the armed forces was wasted, so that there was never the financial stringency which operated elsewhere. Though it must be added that even the German Army had to put up a struggle to separate the money from the civil servants at times. General Dornberger relates an amusing tale of the artifices necessary to obtain vital items for his Weapons Design Office: an indent for 'Appliance for cutting wooden rods, up to 10mm diameter, as per sample' covered the purchase of a pencil sharpener, for example. But for all that, it was still a much easier ambience in which to work, one in which the Army could state its requirements with some confidence in having them met.

And the requirements of the nascent Reichswehr could be summed up in one word – everything. Apart from a 75mm infantry gun introduced in the late 1920s, every artillery piece on the books was of World War One or earlier vintage. They were well behind the current thinking of technical gunmakers, and certainly not up to the requirements of range and mobility which the new apostles of armoured warfare were demanding. But as well as requiring a fresh outfit of standard items – field guns, medium guns, anti-aircraft and anti-tank guns – the army were sufficiently confident in the availability of funds in the future to add some less commonplace items to their shopping list. Railway guns, including ultra-long-range weapons; coast defence guns; self-propelled siege

The German infantry gun 18, the first post-World War One design to enter service.

guns; these were prominent in the list, and there was ample encouragement for the gunmakers to experiment and adopt unorthodox solutions if they felt so inclined.

In the matter of a divisional artillery field-piece, the area which had seen so much debate in Britain, the German Army was equally undecided. During the First World War the field piece had been a 77mm gun and this was, later in the war, augmented by a 105mm howitzer. During the 1920s various trials were conducted in attempts to determine which was the better weapon and which should become the divisional artillery's standard, and by 1930 the 105mm howitzer – actually a gun-howitzer – was selected. Nevertheless the 77mm gun was still highly regarded and it was retained in service, fitted with a new barrel of 75mm calibre, in considerable numbers. The question was never finally settled, and even during the course of the Second World War the debate continued; eventually priorities were reversed and the 75mm gun accepted as the better proposition, new designs being developed after 1943. Yet at the same time fresh models of 105mm howitzer were also under development, as if to take out some form of insurance against the possible failure of the 75mm theories.

The field gun question reveals, in microcosm, the defect of the German weapons development system: that due to ample design talent and a fairly liberal purse, too many ideas were pursued at once. The original intention in the 1920s was to develop a logical series of weapons in which guns and howitzers shared common carriage designs in order to rationalise production and provide an ample armoury of reliable and simple standard weapons. This policy appears to have held good until

One of the development prototypes of the German 105mm field howitzer 18 undergoing ballistic tests at a proving ground. A 75mm L/60 AA gun is at the right.

about 1933, after which politics and tribal warfare crept in. Companies, individuals and branches of the armed services all began empire-building, promoting their own ideas and theories without pausing to ask what the rest of the army or industry were doing, activities which often resulted in manufacturing and design effort going to waste on a weapon which was unacceptable. Perhaps the most flamboyant example of this was Krupp's monstrous 80cm railway gun; by playing on Hitler's love of the enormous and spectacular, it was foisted off to the Army and, after six years work on it, finally became a service weapon. It appears, from what records survived the war, to have fired less than a hundred shells in anger before being abandoned for scrap. It has been reliably estimated that twenty million marks – £1,740,000 at the contemporary rate of exchange – went into the project, which contributed absolutely nothing to the German Army's fighting ability and absorbed money and manpower which could have been put to more profitable use in other fields.

Nevertheless, from the Army's demands there arrived an astonishing number of excellent designs; the trouble was that they were surrounded by an equally astonishing amount of rubbish, and it took time and experience to sort the wheat from the chaff. In some cases the wrong idea was pursued while the good one languished, and only after discovering that the research was fruitless could the developers back-track and start again on the path which eventually proved to be the correct one. Setback to a good many ideas was the famous 'One Year Order' of 1939; this assumed that the war would be victoriously concluded by the end of 1940, and thus any line of development which could not guarantee successful completion to service acceptance standards within that time was arbitrarily guillotined. Another error was the rather off-hand classification of weapons into 'offensive' and 'defensive' types; apart from a few exceptions such as anti-aircraft guns, 'defensive' weapons were frowned on as not being in keeping with the Blitzkrieg spirit. Fortunately this edict had little effect on the production of guns, since these are hard to classify; but the most damaging effects fell on the electronic and missile experimenters, and this, in turn, led to a secondary effect on artillery in that it greatly delayed the adoption of radar and electronic prediction in anti-aircraft fire control applications.

As befitted the nation who were placing their reliance on armoured warfare, the Germans were particularly attentive to the question of providing a potent anti-tank gun. As with most countries, anti-tank defence devolved on the infantry and, as a result, the preferred weapon was a lightweight high-velocity gun of 37mm calibre, powerful enough to pierce the contemporary tank but withal sufficiently light and handy to be easily manoeuvred by a handful of men. But it was obvious that, sooner or later, heavier armour would make its appearance and would have to be countered; the simple answer to that, of course, was to produce a heavier gun, but this meant abandoning the tactical advantages of a lightweight weapon, so other solutions were sought.

In 1904 a German, Karl Puff, patented the idea of using a gun barrel which tapered in calibre from breech to muzzle, together with a projectile capable of being reduced in diameter during its passage through such a barrel. His intention was simply to achieve high velocity, which was done by reason of the base area of the shot decreasing, thus giving an increase in unit pressure of the propelling gas and thus of velocity. Nothing much came of Puff's patent since, like so many patents of the time, it was in advance of the technology available to manufacture it successfully. In the 1920s the idea was looked at afresh by another German engineer named Gerlich. In conjunction with Halbe, a gunsmith, he developed the idea sufficiently to be able to market a number of sporting rifles and special ammunition under the name 'Halger' which embodied the taper-bore principle. He also tried to interest various armies in these weapons as specialised sniping rifles, and in the early 1930s he was briefly employed by both the British and U.S. War Departments on trials with taper-bore rifles.

At the same time, others were making experiments along similar lines, the most notable being those of the Danish 'Ultra' company of Otterup; their work was so impressive that the French Army actually ordered fifty tapered barrels from them, not, it was said by the French, in order to actually build guns for service but simply in order to see whether it was possible to produce taper-bore barrels as a practical and routine manufacturing operation.

The taper-bore gun. The projectile is fitted with skirt driving bands which are squeezed down during the movement up the barrel, so that the shot is ejected with a smooth contour and the reduction in base area gives an increase in velocity.

Gerlich returned to Germany some time in the middle 1930s and his subsequent activities have escaped record. But it seems likely that he was retained as a designer or adviser, since the taper bore was now seized upon as the answer to the problem of how to make lightweight but powerful anti-tank guns. For, all other things being equal, good anti-tank performance relied on high velocity, and for two reasons: firstly because high velocity meant smashing power at the target so as to penetrate the tank's armour; and secondly because high velocity meant a short time of flight from gun to target and a flat trajectory, both of which meant a better chance of hitting the tank with the first shot.

Although work on the taper bore anti-tank guns appears to have begun about 1937, the development of such a revolutionary idea and, in particular, the perfection of the special ammunition to go with it, took time, and it was not until late in 1940 that the guns began to enter service. During this period of development, however, a fresh approach to the problem of defeating armour had been discovered and was under active development.

Early in 1938 the military attaches of various European nations stationed in Switzerland were approached by two Swiss, Professor Matthias and Dr Mohaupt, with the news that they had perfected a new and powerful explosive which was particularly suited to the attack of tanks. A demonstration was to be held in October 1938 after which terms could be discussed for their divulging the secret and licensing the process.

No reports of this demonstration appear to have survived; it has been suggested that it was poorly attended, largely because the military attachés were getting tired of inventors offering New And Powerful Explosives every fortnight. But in January 1939 another demonstration was held in which rifle grenades were fired at 60mm armour plate and succeeded in making holes of 4mm diameter. The inventors claimed that their explosive mixture was easily obtainable and could be produced for no more than sixpence a pound; but there seems to have been some sleight of hand involved. As the British report on the demonstration recorded:

'On the first firing, which gave an Explosion Only [i.e. not an effective detonation] there was a cloud of yellow smoke and a yellow deposit on the ground. Such an effect would be produced by Picric Acid, but there is some suspicion that this was done intentionally in order to give a misleading idea as to the nature of the explosive. Information was subsequently obtained that Dr Mohaupt had been getting TNT from a Swiss explosives company at Dottikon, and this may be a component of the mixture...'

In fact Matthias and Mohaupt had perfected an explosive phenomenon which, as a laboratory experiment – not to say a parlour trick – had been known for some years. In the 1880s an American experi-

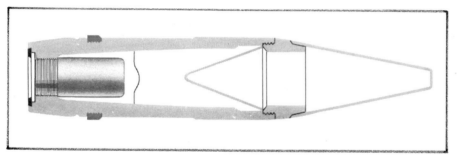

A hollow charge shell for the American 105mm howitzer. The fuze is fitted in the base, since a normal nose fuze could interfere with the action of the penetrating jet. The long empty head provides the required 'stand-off' distance from the target to ensure correct jet formation before striking the armour.

mentor, Monroe, had shown that if an explosive block were hollowed out on the face in contact with a steel plate, after detonation the shape of the hollow would be reproduced in the plate. In 1914 a German scientist, Neumann, published a paper 'Zeitschrift für das Gesamte Schiess und Sprengstoffwesen' (Vol 9, p183) in which he advocated fitting a metal lining to the cavity; this increased the effect to the point where the detonation would now hole the plate. During the course of the First World War numerous experimenters were drawn to the 'Monroe Effect' or 'Neumann Effect' and attempted to turn it to practical account as a weapon, though without much success. The Swiss gentlemen had simply worked on Neuman's theories and perfected them; unfortunately for them, so had other people. The British report continues:

'. . . the Research Department representatives then explained that the Research Department of Woolwich Arsenal had been able, by methods which had been known for many years, to produce results on trials which strongly resembled those obtained by Mohaupt. Photographs were shown illustrating these results, and these were so close to Mohaupt's that he could not but admit that the effects were identical . . . . He was obviously taken aback at the results shown . . . .'

The Neumann Effect or 'Hollow Charge' as it came to be universally known, became a viable weapon of war from then on. We do not know how many other powers were approached by Matthias and Mohaupt, but certainly their activities stimulated interest in the half-forgotten phenomenon in Britain and doubtless in Germany too. The advantage of the hollow charge projectile lay in that its effects appeared to be independent of velocity; while it was still desirable to have a high velocity in order to reap the benefits of short time of flight and flat trajectory, there was now no need to take it beyond the point of ensuring these in order to achieve a higher striking velocity for the sake of penetration. Provided a reasonable velocity could be obtained, any gun could use a hollow charge projectile, capable of penetrating any tank then known or even contemplated.

The arrival of the hollow charge was timely; no longer need anti-tank guns have the sole responsibility for anti-tank defence; any gun now had the ability to cope with armour. Furthermore, as the war progressed, the

In spite of the 'Blitz-krieg' image, much of the German artillery was horse-drawn and remained so throughout the war.

Germans found difficulties in the way of developing taper-bore weapons, and their eventual decision to give them up was made more palatable because of the availability of hollow charge munitions to fill what would otherwise have been a nasty hole in their defensive line-up.

One minor feature of German artillery deserves mention: its transportation. Although the Army was mechanisation-conscious, this seems to have extended little further than the Panzer Divisions, for the artillery of the infantry division was still horse-drawn in 1939 and much of it remained horse-drawn throughout the war. It seems difficult to reconcile this with the 'Blitzkrieg' image, but it seems likely to have been due to two factors: one, the difficulty of producing sufficient numbers of specialised artillery tractors – for nothing which was commercially available was suited to this task – and secondly to the critical problem of Germany's oil supplies, imports which had to be parcelled out carefully between the various arms of the services. The economy in oil derived from horse-drawn artillery was of a significant degree.

Chapter 2
WAR

When Britain and France declared war on Germany in 1939 the immediate reaction was virtually to take up where things had been left in 1918, and as a result a new 'Western Front' was formed, using the Maginot Line as its basis. The British artillery consisted, for the most part, of slightly improved versions of the weapons which had seen action on the same front in the previous war; the only visible result of all the debate and research of the intervening years was a handful of the new 25-pounder guns – though in fact these were no more than 25-pounder barrels inserted into elderly 18-pounder carriages, an economy measure decreed by the need to use up the large numbers of serviceable carriages which were in store. It was a second-best expedient, since the carriage design prevented the full ballistic potential of the barrel being realised, and instead of the 13,400 yard range of which the gun was capable, the 18/25-pounder (as it was commonly called) could only reach to 11,800 yards. The remainder of the artillery strength was composed of such veterans as the 60-pounder (introduced in 1904), the 4.5-inch howitzer (also 1904), the 8-inch howitzer (1915), the 9.2-inch howitzer (1914) and the 12-inch howitzer (1916).

The British 60-pounder gun. Obsolete and cumbersome, it had to serve until something more modern appeared, and the final models (with pneumatic tyres) were not declared obsolete until August 1944.

A 12-inch howitzer in action in France in 1940. Due to the speed of the German advance and the evacuation from Dunkirk all these superheavy guns were left behind.

The French 105mm M35 howitzer. With a range of 11,250 yards and a 34.5lb shell, this was the best field piece the French owned, but there were not enough of them available.

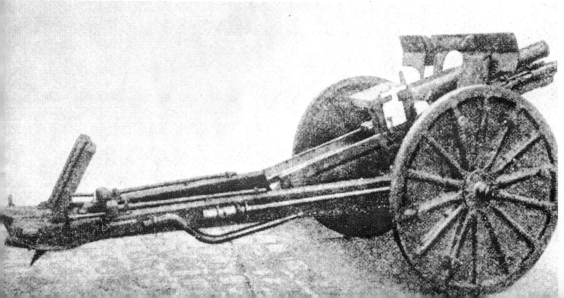

The French were, if anything, worse off, since they still pinned their faith on the 1897 model 75mm gun, though like most of the British designs this weapon had been improved in the interval by the addition of pneumatic tyres and better ammunition, so that its maximum range had been increased to 12,500 yards – though the shell was still pitifully small. A far better weapon was their 105mm M1935 howitzer, of which about 400 were available by 1939; which meant that only one battery of each of the divisional artillery regiments was equipped with a modern weapon. The principal French reliance was, of course, on the permanent guns of the Maginot Line, but the majority of these were elderly designs which in many respects vitiated the sophisticated fortresses in which they were mounted.

When the 'sitzkrieg' finally ended on that fateful day in May 1940, the war of movement which followed was in the best British tradition of 'starting every war with a disastrous retreat, and it was a far cry from the organised leap-frogging of batteries which peacetime training had laid down as the normal 'fire and movement' support of a moving front. Some of the post-battle reports by British artillery officers illuminate the peculiar situation:

'The fighting started with one troop firing over open sights while the remainder of the battery packed up and departed at a speed well up to Horse Artillery standards, though the technique might have called for comments from the Instructors-in-Gunnery at Larkhill . . . .'

Not the least of their worries was the stream of refugees on the roads of France and Belgium:

'On the second occasion very short notice to withdraw was received, the roads were hopelessly blocked with civilian and military traffic, and some hours after the battery should have withdrawn we were still waiting for the tractors. They arrived shortly before the leading German troops . . . .'

The speed of the German advance, compounded by the rapid collapse of the French and Belgian Armies, came as an unpleasant surprise to soldiers who were accustomed to having a buffer zone between them and the actual line of combat and who were therefore inclined to take their time:

'To my horror and amazement I found our last infantry emerging from the forest and tumbling back towards the guns, and as yet no reports of "closing down" from the battery. I dashed back to the nearest troop and found every kind of junk being slowly loaded on to the waiting tractors (stuff which might have been of use in a "Thirty Years' War" but certainly not in this), and no conception at all of what was required in a rearguard action . . . .'

Certain points which had been held in doubt in pre-war days now resolved themselves; one was the wisdom of the Royal Artillery in mechanising. In spite of the chaos, fuel always seemed to appear when it was needed, and the flexibility and speed of a mechanised regiment allowed sub-units to detour by different routes and rendezvous at a pre-arranged point with remarkable reliability. The contrast between this and the sorry plight of the French horse-drawn batteries under aerial attack, short of fodder, and attempting to thread a way through the congestion on the roads was most marked. The other significant point was the ability to control a scattered regiment and bring it together by radio communication:

'It was only the wireless signal, travelling in its mysterious way, that could find its destination, and without it none of the component parts of the regiment would have known where the others were in that complicated country. It was quite miraculous how the situation sorted itself out by wireless . . . .'

British troops in France manning a 25mm Hotchkiss anti-tank gun, one of the least effective of its class. Of French origin, a quantity were bought by Britain in 1938 to supplement the supply of two-pounders. Most were left in France and the rest were scrapped when their ammunition stock was exhausted.

However, another report spoke of the difficulties of trying to contact and control 'as many as seven radio sets on one frequency', a remark indicative of the relative novelty of a radio network. Five years later forty or more sets would be working on the same frequency, perfectly controlled and controllable. Although radio was seen to be the absolute solution to the communication and control problem, it got off to a bad start in France. The phoney war period, with gun batteries well dug in, had proliferated telephone communication at the expense of radio, largely on the grounds of security – a telephone being harder to tap than

a radio signal was to overhear. For most of the time prior to the German attack there had been a general prohibition on the use of radio, and much of the Army had been happy to obey; many of the men were reservists or men lately returned from overseas stations, and had little experience with radio, and a policy of radio silence suited them very well. But a few units – one or two artillery regiments among them – risked the wrath of the All-Highest and maintained their radio communications in working order, practising operators and maintenance men at every opportunity. Their forethought paid a massive dividend; the quotation above, relating to the use of radio to keep a scattered regiment together, was from one of these units. But those who had stuck to the telephone, relying on the radio to be 'all right on the night' found themselves enveloped in silence once they began to move.

The losses in guns left behind in the evacuation of the BEF were enormous, but, in retrospect, mostly beneficial. The field regiments had been equipped with the 25-pounder Mark One (the correct name for the 18/25 pounder) but the Mark Two equipment, based on a carriage design taken from the Vickers 4.1-inch howitzer of 1930 and allowing the gun to reach its full 13,400 yard range, had begun to come off the production lines; the first to see action were used in the short Norway campaign. The heavy and super-heavy weapons, 8-inch, 9.2-inch and 12-inch howitzers and guns in both road and railway versions which were left behind formed a large portion of the available stocks, as did the medium guns, so that here was another incentive to put more modern designs into production rather than continue to make do with the older weapons, which would otherwise, without any doubt, have been the case. Only in the anti-tank guns did the Dunkirk losses have a far-reaching and ill effect; 509 two-pounder guns were left behind in France

A German 15cm K39 medium gun in France, 1940. Originally destined for Turkey, these guns were taken over by the German Army on the outbreak of war. Firing a 94lb shell to 27,000 yards, it could also be emplaced on a special platform as a coast-defence gun.

and Belgium and, with a German invasion expected hourly, anti-tank guns were obviously high on the replacement priority list.

The two-pounder had performed reasonably well in France, but the need for a heavier gun as a replacement for it had long been appreciated. In 1938 a design of six-pounder had been put on paper but had been shelved, since the two-pounder was quite adequate at that time and there were other, more pressing, demands on the gun-making factories. In the summer of 1940 the six-pounder was put forward as the obvious replacement for the lost two-pounders and immediately propounded a dilemma: while the six-pounder was, on paper, the superior weapon, it was an unknown quantity. Pilot models would have to be made, trials carried out, modifications made, more trials, and finally production facilities laid out before any guns would be available to the troops. On the other hand, the two-pounder, although approaching the end of its useful life and far inferior to the promised performance of the six-pounder, was a known quantity; it worked, the troops were familiar with it, and production capacity for the gun and its ammunition existed and was functioning. A bird in the hand was worth two in the bush in those desperate days, and the production of the two-pounder was therefore continued while the six-pounder was put to one side, a decision which, justifiable though it was at the time, was to bring disaster extremely close in the Western Desert.

Fortunately not all the problems facing the Royal Artillery were quite as fundamental or as difficult as that one; most of them were at a lower

The two-pounder anti-tank gun, wheels removed, on its tripod mounting which allowed 360° of traverse. An elegant weapon of great precision and mechanical refinement, but difficult to make and its performance was soon overtaken by improvements in tank design.

level and concerned organisation and handling of the guns in the light of what had been learned in France. The worth of radio having been proven, its use was extended, a practice which led to new techniques of operating; with ten or a dozen or more stations on the same 'net' or frequency, rigid discipline and control had to be enforced in order to prevent bedlam from breaking loose. The prime rule was that fire orders – instructions from an observer to the guns to engage a target – were sacrosanct; the cry of 'Hello 25, Fire Orders, Over' immediately stilled any chatter about ration returns, demands for boots or other administrative affairs, and no station could speak on the air until the shoot was completed. Obviously, if another observer on the same net needed to do so, he could pass fire orders to another gun troop to engage another target, the two sets of operators taking it in turn to get their orders through.

Next for consideration came organisation; in 1938 the field branch artillery had been re-organised along ill-considered lines, as a result of which the field regiment of 24 guns was split into two 12-gun batteries each of three 4-gun troops. The remarkable thing about this re-organisation is that no-one, to this day, knows how or where the idea originated; it certainly didn't originate within the Royal Artillery, who were less than pleased at having to implement it. There was, of course, more to it than a simple division of guns – it involved changes in staffing and fire control and several other upsetting features. But the basic flaw lay in the division of guns, since the field regiment was supposed to support an infantry brigade, and a brigade contained three battalions; splitting two batteries between three battalions was impossible, so the regiment, while retaining 24 guns, was now re-organised on a three-battery basis, each battery of eight guns being split into two four-gun troops.

The last major task was the marriage of these two basics – organisation and communication – in such a fashion as to permit a degree of control which would allow massive firepower to be brought to bear on a target from as many guns as were available or thought necessary. In theory it was perfectly feasible as the system stood; an observer seeing a target could communicate with his own troop and open fire. If he felt the target demanded more attention he could request the fire of both troops of his battery. If more metal was warranted, the battery could, on another radio frequency, call for the fire of the entire regiment, passing information on the target location to the adjutant who, in turn, passed it to the other batteries. The adjutant could also pass this information back to division and, through them obtain the fire of the other regiments in the divisional area. Obviously all this passing of information to and fro took time, time in which the target might well have thought better of it and gone home. What was needed was a channel of communication which would cut out the repetition and a fire control system which would permit rapid response.

This was eventually achieved in 1941 by Brigadier (later Major-General) J. H. Parham, then Commanding Royal Artillery 38th Division. He arranged for a Divisional Observation Post manned by a 'CRA's Representative' to be in direct communication with divisional HQ, who could then re-transmit his orders direct to the various regiments. Allied with this came a faster system of plotting the target and deducing gun data; this system was distinctly counter to pre-war training which had extolled accuracy as being preferable to speed, but as was pointed out at the time, the minor inaccuracies due to the new system were swallowed up in the spread of fire of a whole division's guns. It must be said that the method as first devised strayed a little too far from the desirable degree of accuracy in that it failed to take into account a basic defect in the plotting system; plotting was done on a large sheet of paper printed with a 1/25,000 scale grid, and within a few hours of being printed the paper would stretch or shrink, depending upon the humidity, thus throwing out the relationship of the printed lines. Once this was discovered and a system of plotting devised to neutralize it, accuracy increased considerably. Beginning as a system for firing all the guns of a division, it was soon extended to cover all Corps and eventually Army artillery within range of the target, and apart from a few modifications to cater for improved equipment it is still in use today.

The idea of a special 'CRA's Rep.' was soon abandoned when it was seen that the normal observation post officers were perfectly well able to assess the worth of a target and call for the appropriate gun strength, though, strictly speaking, they had to receive confirmation from higher formation before they could open fire. Such confirmation was never withheld unless some of the desired guns were already engaged on a task of greater importance. The greatest advantage the system bestowed, however, was the speed of response; a call for the regimental strength was answered by ranging fire within a minute once the system was mastered, and a call for the divisional guns usually had the entire 72 guns laid on target and ready to fire in less than three minutes.

While the field artillery were putting their house in order for the future, the rest of the nation were more apprehensive about the present. The Wehrmacht stood on the cliffs of Calais while invasion barges were being assembled in the harbours of Belgium and France. England had to be turned into an armed camp ready to throw the threatened invasion back into the sea, and for this guns were needed, both for fixed defences and to equip the mobile army whose guns had been left behind at Dunkirk. For the latter the production of 25-pounders was stepped up and, as an interim measure, stocks of the obsolescent 18-pounder were turned out and refurbished. In addition several hundred equally obsolescent 75mm guns were purchased from the United States, the last of the M1916, M1917 and French M1897 produced on First World War contracts, together with a stock of antedeluvian ammunition to suit.

For the provision of fixed defences on the beaches, anything which could shoot was deemed serviceable and issued. Every spare coast defence gun and mounting was put to use, but this covered little, and the Royal Navy were approached for help. They, with commendable thrift and forethought, had stored away every gun removed from every ship scrapped since 1918 and this collection was now raided for anything which could be used in a defensive application. The principal problem was that of emplacing the weapons, since they were all on shipboard patterns of mounting, but with great ingenuity a wide selection of ground platforms were improvised and produced at short notice. Guns were bolted down to concrete slabs, to platforms of railway sleepers or wooden baulks, even to boilerplate platforms anchored in concrete and brick foundations. Some of the lighter weapons were assembled to commandeered motor trucks to form a mobile reserve. Shields of various kinds were hurriedly designed and locally manufactured to suit whatever gun happened to be issued. By October 1940 a total of 510 guns had been loaned by the Royal Navy and were in place, a collection of 143 6-inch, 30 4.7-inch, 245 4-inch, 48 12-pounder, and 24 three-pounder of different marks and patterns. Guns were still being turned out of odd corners in 1941; one of the most unusual sources was the removal of 27 138mm guns from the ex-French warships *Courbet* and *Paris*. These were handed over to the War Office who, wise in the ways of the world, promptly had them inspected, revealing that they were all worn to the limit of their usefulness; one, indeed, was so worn as not to reveal any vestige of rifling in its bore. What with that and the small amount of ammunition available for the guns, very few of these weapons were actually put to use.

Railway guns and howitzers were also brought back into use, being deployed on sidings along the south coast so as to be ready to bombard likely invasion beaches. Among these was the Army's solitary 18-inch railway howitzer, which was located on a stretch of disused railway line in Kent from which it could cover most of the shore line from Margate to Rye. The Dover area was, naturally, at high risk, and due to its closeness to France it was soon under fire from German long range guns. By way of retaliation three old railway mountings dating from 1918 were resurrected, fitted with 13.5-inch naval guns and, manned by Royal Marines, sent to Dover as a first instalment. Plans were then put in hand for the mounting of a variety of other heavy guns both for bombarding France and in order to close the Straits of Dover to enemy shipping.

It was the anti-aircraft gunners who had the most difficult task, since there was no such doubt about the impending arrival of the Luftwaffe as there was about that of the Wehrmacht. Once again, numerous elderly weapons were brought out of retirement to augment the modern

1940 saw the deployment of the remaining British railway guns to cover possible invasion beaches. Here a 12-inch howitzer is being emplaced.

Loading the US 155mm Howitzer M1918. Two men are ramming the 95lb shell into the breech, and this will be followed by the bagged charge. On the right a cannoneer waits to close the breech, while on the left the gunner is setting the sights.

His Majesty's Gun
'Gladiator', a 13.5-
inch manned by
Royal Marines, fires
a 1,250lb shell across
the Channel from its
position near Dover
in March 1943.

September 1939 and
an elderly 3-inch
20cwt anti-aircraft
gun on a Peerless
lorry, of 1918
vintage, takes up
position in Parlia-
ment Square.

armament, but it seems that the majority of these museum pieces were seen less as a viable form of defence than as a method of cheering up the populace. I know of one town close to London where a three-inch gun on motor truck mounting, manned by Naval ratings, had the task of touring round during air raids, driving rapidly from one air-raid shelter to another. At each shelter the gun would halt and loose two or three rounds into the sky at random in order to hearten the shelterers with the sound of active retaliation. With no fire control instruments and simply firing over open sights, no-one was more surprised than the gunners themselves when, one night, they brought down a German bomber by a chance shot.

Fortunately the greater part of the air defences were better equipped than that; the 3-inch 20cwt of First War vintage was still in service in large numbers, but the new 3.7-inch gun had high priority and was coming from the factories at an increasing rate. In some locations, where Naval ammunition supplies could be provided, 4.5-inch guns were installed, while the 40mm Bofors, originally bought from Sweden and then built in Britain under licence, was a formidable deterrent to low-flyers and, as much as anything, the reason for the later German abandonment of the dive-bomber technique.

Fire control was, of course, the great stumbling block to an effective air defence, particularly at night. Apart from early warning and relatively coarse pointing from sound locators, all methods of target acquisition and tracking relied on optical aids. By day these could be negated by cloud and by night they relied on searchlights to illuminate the target. But by the end of 1940 radar had made great strides and was gradually being assimilated into the gun defences. The RAF Chain Home coastal radars were able to detect German bombing fleets as they assembled over the continent and thus give far better warning than could acoustics, and early types of gun control radar sets were making their appearance. These were primitive devices using enormous aerials (since wave-lengths were still measured in metres) and required a cumbrous ground mat of wire mesh to be laid around the set to act as a signal reflector, but they worked reasonably well and gave promise of better things to come. With this assistance, anti-aircraft could now detect targets in darkness or through cloud, if not with gun-shot accuracy, at least with sufficient accuracy to allow a barrage of fire to be discharged in the right direction and at approximately the right height.

While the Army were engaged in organising the defences and the munition factories in stepping up production, the inventors were having a field day dreaming up new (to them) and fearful (usually to the potential user) weapons, and the Ordnance Board obtained some light relief from serious matters by examining and rejecting them. A sample of a hoary old idea which gets taken out and shaken from time to time was 'A Shell Containing Bolas' proposed by an American: 'This invention consists of a number of weights, eccentric to the axis of the shell, connected by wires coiled within the body of the shell. On the operation of a time fuze the head and base of the shell are blown off and the spin of the system causes the weights to move outwards thus uncoiling the wires, until the ultimate form is that of South American Bolas ... the diameter is estimated to be 250 feet ...' It was, perhaps, better thought out than the hosts of similar suggestions which had been put up in 1915-18, but examination showed that the flying weights could not develop sufficient inertia to damage an aircraft; the idea was politely rejected.

Another idea deserves mention; a proposal by a Mr Clementi for a multiple-chambered gun: '... a super-velocity gun in which a multiple charge is loaded into a number of separate chambers. The charges are fired at intervals as the projectile proceeds down the gun and the propulsive forces on the projectile are thus maintained ...' Now, this idea had first appeared in the 1870s and had re-appeared at frequent intervals thereafter, whenever some fresh inventor had fastened on to it; it was nothing new to the Ordnance Board. 'The idea behind such inventions, though attractive theoretically, is of value only insofar as its practical application is possible ...' and the Board proceeded to explain the inherent difficulties, the principal of which was the impossibility of igniting the auxiliary charges with the degree of precise timing necessary for the weapon to function in accordance with the theory. The multiple-chambered gun was turned down flat; yet, at this same time, the same idea appeared in Germany from another inventor, was seized upon and, as will be later explained, occupied a vast amount of men, machinery and money for the next five years without producing any worthwhile results.

It might be said here that many critics, in the postwar years, castigated the Ordnance Board unmercifully for being reactionary and resistant to new ideas. Examination of their 'Proceedings' will reveal that this is far from true; very few good ideas were ever overlooked by the Board, and the inventions which were brought into service against their advice or without their knowledge invariably finished up in front of them to be re-worked into practical weapons. The point was that the Board had accumulated a vast amount of knowledge of what was and was not feasible in a weapons context, and when such ideas as the multiple-chambered gun came before them they were able to point out previous attempts at the same thing and, in effect, ask the inventor just how his proposal was anticipated to be any better than those which had failed before. It is apposite to recall the remark reputed to have come from a member of the Board at the turn of the century when, asked by a gunmaker why so many ideas were turned down, replied: 'If we only make *one* mistake out of every hundred decisions that we give, it will be acknowledged that we do remarkably well. Ninety-nine inventions out of every hundred submitted are worthless. We shall, therefore, do remarkably well if we condemn them all.' He doubtless had his tongue in the cheek when he said it, but there was, all the same, a grain of truth in it.

While the occupants of Britain laboured to produce weapons, train on them, and gradually put the fear of invasion behind them, the war continued in other places, and so far as Britain was concerned the seat of war was in the Western Desert.

The actions of the British armies in the Western desert can be depicted as a sine curve, beginning with outstanding success, descending to abysmal defeats, and finally returning to a victorious crest. The whys and wherefores of this have been passionately argued ever since, and it is no part of my brief to provide yet another analysis; our interest lies in artillery. But the fact remains that the graph of British fortunes in the desert can be paralleled by another graph labelled 'Handling of Artillery in Accordance with Doctrine'. When the guns were properly used, in the manner laid down by the teachings of the School of Artillery, the army prospered. When they were mishandled, the army suffered. This may be an over-simplification, and the equation might be equally well reversed to say that when the army prospered the artillery was correctly used; but whichever the cause and whichever the effect, the correlation is inescapable.

Precisely how this came about is difficult to pin-point, but it has a great deal to do with the Eighth Army's peculiar position in the war. It was fighting in an area devoid of any restrictions such as railways, rivers, mountain ranges or cities; it was fighting a long way from home and the Schools of Instruction; it was fighting in an area where the normal rules appeared not to apply or at least to have little relevance; but above all, it was fighting – which was more than any other British army appeared to be doing at that time. As a result, the Eighth Army rather became a law unto itself; the theory that special conditions warrant special methods became an article of faith, eccentricity thrived, and orthodox methods tended to be dismissed as '1918 thinking'.

When the desert campaign began, orthodoxy reigned and Wavell's operations against the Italian Army in 1940-41 were masterpieces of text-book soldiering, yet leavened with a degree of dash and flair which showed that conducting battles in the approved manner still left room for individual initiative.

But with the arrival of German reinforcements to stiffen the Italian resistance, some unaccountable urge to decentralise struck the Eighth Army. It became a credo that the division, that normal autonomous military formation, was too cumbersome and unwieldy to be controlled in a desert environment; why this peculiar belief should have been given credence is difficult to ascertain with any reliability and even more difficult to understand. It has been suggested that it came about as a

result of the autumn and winter operations of 1941, the poor British showing in which convinced Auchinleck to begin the move to the 'Brigade Group' concept. The division remained in name only, the erstwhile divisional headquarters being the only component to carry on as before. The rest was now chopped in three to form three brigade groups, so that the nucleus of each was the infantry brigade and the fire support was one field regiment, plus one-third of whatever other artillery the division happened to have had.

The Siege of Tobruk, 1941, with the 60-pounder still in action.

Having thus obtained three autonomous units for the price of one, the tendency was to credit them with far more ability than was actually present and give them tasks in battle which should properly have been performed by a division. On paper the system produced a large number of independent formations, but on the ground the results were less happy; so far as artillery was concerned it meant that the sole support of the group was now the field regiment's 24 guns, and the carefully-built structure which enabled more weapons to be brought into play when needed had been demolished. Since the groups generally operated miles away from each other, fire support from the rest of the division no longer existed, and the Brigade Group sank or swam on the efforts of its own artillery alone.

This might not have been so bad had the field guns been able to concern themselves solely with the normal and traditional type of indirect supporting fire; but at this juncture the earlier controversy over

Italian gunners in
Cyrenaica manning
a 149mm gun. Note
that in spite of its
size a brass cartridge
case is used.

Italian gunners in Cyrenaica manning a 149mm gun. Note that in spite of its size a brass cartridge case is used.

the production of two-pounders or six-pounders bore its bitter fruit. The standard anti-tank gun was the two-pounder, assisted by a handful of 37mm Bofors anti-tank guns which had been bought by the Sudan Government in 1939. The two-pounder was the better of the two, but even it was past the peak of its usefulness; its penetration, using a solid steel shot, was 50mm of plate at 1,000 yards range, and solid steel shot was the only ammunition it had. The German tanks, on the other hand, were armed with 50mm and 75mm guns; the 50mm had a slightly better penetration than did the two-pounder, while the 75mm could pierce 94mm at 1,000 yards. More to the point though was the fact that both these guns were liberally provided with high explosive shells, so that they could stand away at long range, at which their armour was impervious to the two-pounder, and shell the anti-tank gun into submission at their leisure. The only counter to this was more cunning siting of the two-pounders in order to try and ambush the tanks at short range, but that gave only marginal improvements. The real solution was to 'borrow' the field battery's 25-pounder; this fired a 20lb steel shot which although in theory only slightly more penetrative than the two-pounder, in fact delivered a more telling blow and had a longer effective reach. Moreover it had an efficient high explosive shell which was not to be spurned as a long-range weapon for dealing with tanks if they tried

their stand-off tactics. In consequence the field guns had to be deployed in positions where they could form an anti-tank defence to the Brigade Group as well as fire their normal supporting role, and thus the guns usually took the brunt of the German attacks. They were often so busy shooting at tanks that they had little time or opportunity for other things.

With the arrival of the six-pounder anti-tank gun the balance was restored and the Panzers found life a little less carefree. Australians in the Desert, 1942.

Another splintering system was the invention of the 'Jock Column' by Brigadier 'Jock' Campbell, VC. In this, a mobile column formed from whatever happened to be available in the way of armoured cars and lorried infantry, 'supported' by a troop of field artillery, would sally forth into the desert as a mobile reconnaisance and raiding force. While it was thus restricted in purpose the 'column' was no bad thing, though affairs frequently went awry:

'We came into action in the dark, not knowing where the enemy were. At dawn I sent out OPs (observation post parties) who at first light saw tanks moving down towards us. We shelled them at long range, but stopped when the range shortened to 5,000 yards or so, so as not to give our position away, and waited to deal with them over open sights. To our consternation they turned out to be one of our own cavalry regiments, but fortunately we had not done any damage. They were not very pleased . . .'

But the column theory got out of hand and columns began to be despatched into the face of far superior forces apparently for no better reason than to be seen to be doing something. One such column, made up of two infantry battalions, a field battery and a squadron of light tanks, was sent out to cut 200 miles across the desert south of Benghazi to harrass and cut off the German retreat in December 1941; it was so unwise as to spend a night in a location from which the guns had fired during the day, instead of withdrawing into the desert as was the rule. It paid the price by suffering an attack by thirty German tanks at dawn. The artillery was completely destroyed and the column scattered to the four winds. This happened more and more frequently until it was gradually realised that the days of carefree columns were over when the Germans took to scouring the desert with tanks.

German use of artillery, on the other hand, rarely diverged from their normal practices insofar as field artillery went. But where they particularly made their mark was in the bold and effective handling of their anti-tank artillery, and the addition to it of a new dimension in the 88mm gun, a weapon which soon gathered to itself a reputation for superiority and invincibility which was not entirely justified.

The 88mm Flak Model 18 was the standard German medium anti-

The arrival of the six-pounder meant that 25-pounders could get back to their proper job of field artillery. Notice the discarded propelling charge sections lying on top of the sandbags.

The German 88mm Flak 18 anti-aircraft gun, frequently employed as an anti-tank weapon. The difficulty of concealing it can be judged from this picture.

aircraft gun and, having been in production since 1933, there were a lot of them in service. During the Spanish Civil War some had been taken to Spain by the Kondor Legion and, once or twice, they were used as anti-tank guns. If any foreign observers ever noticed this employment, it was put down to the heat of the moment and never considered to be a workable doctrine. The Germans, though, appreciated the power of the gun in this role, and produced a specialised anti-tank shell for the weapon; indeed, this application of the 88mm gun seems to have been the starting point for their later policy of providing anti-tank ammunition for every weapon, irrespective of its primary role, basing their decision on various minor actions in Spain which pointed to the fact that tanks might well appear anywhere on the battlefield, evading the specialist anti-tank guns, and might have to be dealt with by any artillery unit. (This policy, incidentally, does seem to have been carried to extremes in some cases; even the 128mm twin anti-aircraft guns mounted on Flak Towers in the major German cities had their allocation of anti-tank shells.)

Further, the policy of assimilating the fire of the 88mm gun into ground action was laid down before the war began. 'Procedures for the Attack of Fortified Defensive Positions', an official German Army training manual issued in the summer of 1939, said '... assault detachments, closely followed by anti-tank and 88mm guns, will be thrust through any gap in the defensive front . . .' But the 88 saw little use in 1939-40, since the speed of the German movement rarely allowed the sort of manoeuvre envisaged in the manual and because the standard 37mm anti-tank gun was capable of handling most of the armour met by the Germans. An exception was the British tank attack at Arras, when the heavy protection of the Matilda tank caused some raised eyebrows among the German gunners, and a series of trials were conducted against captured specimens, which led to the 88mm gun being brought to people's attention as a potential anti-tank gun should something heavy be needed.

It was not until the Desert campaign that the need arose, and it was largely the open space warfare which gave the gun its chance. In the close conditions of European war it was quite possible to hide an anti-tank gun so that it could withhold its fire until the tank was within two or three hundred yards, and success, even with small calibres, was fairly assured at that sort of range. But in the featureless desert this was almost impossible and, as the British discovered with the two-pounder, close shots rarely happened; the tank usually spotted the gun a long way off and began shelling before he was within lethal range. The same thing applied to British tanks which, due to their lack of high explosive shell, could not duel on the same terms with their German opposite numbers; they could still spot a German anti-tank gun, perhaps pepper it with shot or machine-gun fire or sheer off in some other direction. In this situation the enormous reach and formidable punch of the 88mm was of inestimable value; firing a 21lb piercing shell at 2,600 feet a second, it could penetrate 105mm of plate at 1,000 yards, striking at a 30° angle to the plate. As if that were not enough it also had a tungsten-cored shot, the Panzergranate 40, which weighed 16½lbs and moved at 3,075ft/sec. Due to ballistic deficiencies of the light shot, its performance at 1,000 yards was no better than the standard shell, but at shorter ranges it was deadly, penetrating 126mm at 500 yards. Finally a hollow-charge shell had been provided, capable of holing 165mm of plate at any range, and the maximum ground range of the 88 was in excess of 16,000 metres. Quite literally, what it could see, it could kill.

All this made the 88 very dangerous indeed, and with a reasonable degree of air superiority it made sense to take some of the division's 24 guns and redistribute them as anti-tank guns, reinforcing the normal screen of 12 50mm and 12 37mm guns. The first appearance of the 88 was outside Tobruk, on 14 April 1942, when a number of 'long-barrelled guns on strange carriages' were seen behind the attacking infantry. They did not come into action, and it seems likely that they were awaiting the provision of a suitable gap in order to be thrust in, in accordance with the training manual quoted above. Their first action appears to have been the defence of the Halfaya Pass against the British attack known as

'Battleaxe' in the following June, when 90 British tanks were destroyed, the majority by the fire of a battery of dug-in 88mm guns.

For all its ballistic superiority, the 88 was, by comparison with existing anti-tank guns, an enormous and cumbersome equipment; it stood 6ft 10½inches high and weighed almost five tons when in action. Due to its role as an anti-aircraft gun it was mounted on a four-wheeled platform with outriggers, the wheels being removed when emplacing the gun, and it needed a pit 19 feet long and 17 feet wide to conceal it. Nevertheless, concealed it frequently was, in highly effective fashion, often being dug in on a forward slope and well camouflaged. In emergencies it could be fired off its wheels, and it was boldly handled in this manner when the need arose, frequently being driven out to a flank during an attack and coming into action at ranges of 1,500 or 2,000 yards, to take the attacking tanks in enfilade and do great execution. By the end of 1942 the German Afrika Korps had 86 of these weapons deployed in the anti-tank role.

The question frequently asked at this point is 'Why did the British Army not use their 3.7-inch anti-aircraft gun in a similar fashion?' On the face of it, a reasonable question; the 3.7-inch was the comparable British weapon, on a similar mounting and with a better performance than the 88 in every respect – range, weight of shell, ceiling, penetration

The Italians in Cyrenaica were among the first people to employ their anti-aircraft guns as high velocity, long-range field artillery. This 90mm Ansaldo gun fired a 23lb shell to 19,000 yards, a most useful performance.

and rate of fire. But three things militated against its use as an anti-tank gun: firstly it was a much more technically advanced design than the 88, having been built for electrical data transmission for Case III laying and with no provision for fitting optical sights for ground firing. This meant that before direct shooting could be attempted, some form of sight had to be designed, made and fitted. Secondly there was no anti-tank ammunition for it; the only projectile available at the time was a time-fuzed high explosive shell intended for anti-aircraft firing. And thirdly the number of guns in the Middle East was so small that to provide any for the field army would have meant leaving a gap in the defences of the Suez Canal, a step which was unthinkable.

Nevertheless it was tried; in June 1942 four 3.7-inch anti-aircraft guns with extempore ground sights suddenly arrived at the front, and from the surviving accounts, one wonders who was the more surprised, the anti-aircraft gunners who suddenly found themselves so employed or the occupants of the nest in the desert into which these cuckoos descended. The area to which they were despatched was a depression about half a mile long by a quarter wide, already stuffed to bursting point with four companies of infantry, three field batteries, an anti-tank battery and two light anti-aircraft troops armed with Bofors guns. The commander of this strongpoint promptly sent two of the 3.7s back whence they had come, simply because there was no room for them. The other two stayed, but the location never came under attack and eventually the 3.7s departed as mysteriously as they had come. So ends the story of the first, last and only appearance of the 3.7-inch AA gun as an anti-tank gun in the Western Desert.

A much-travelled warrior; a Soviet 76.2mm field gun captured by the Germans in Russia, converted by them to an anti-tank gun and shipped to North Africa, now captured by the Eighth Army.

Another interesting facet of the German anti-tank effort in the Western Desert was their adoption of large numbers of a captured Russian gun, the 76.2mm Divisional Gun M1936. These, the standard Soviet field gun at the outbreak of war, were swept up in immense numbers in the early days of the German invasion of Russia – in the Smolensk area alone the Germans claimed to have captured over 3,000 guns and howitzers. Even allowing for victor's optimism, the haul across the entire front was still sufficiently large to make it worthwhile to re-furbish the captured weapons and re-issue them. So many of the M 1936 type were taken that it was modified to German standards by adding a muzzle brake, reaming out the chamber to the dimensions of a standard-production German cartridge case, and altering the sighting and laying arrangements to allow one-man gunlaying. So altered, and with German designed and manufactured ammunition, it became the 76.2mm PAK (Panzer Abwehr Kanone) 36(r), and batches of them were shipped to North Africa. It proved to be a formidable weapon; like most Soviet designs it was a light equipment compared to its contemporaries of equal power, and its performance against armour was excellent. With the standard piercing shell the gun could defeat 108mm at 1,000 yards, while the provision of a tungsten-cored shot improved this to 130mm with, as usual, much greater proportional increase at shorter ranges. Since it was originally designed as a field gun it still possessed this capability, firing a 14lb shell to 9,800 yards; in its original Soviet form its maximum range had been 14,800 yards, but the German modifications restricted the maximum elevation and this cut down the range available.

Eventually the 'Benghazi Handicaps', as the alternate advances and retreats across the Desert were facetiously known, came to an end with the holding of the German advance at Alamein, and with this stand came a return to orthodoxy and sanity in artillery employment with the Eighth Army. The holding position was backed up by field and medium artillery properly deployed, for now the six-pounder anti-tank gun had arrived to relieve the field guns of their responsibility in that sphere, the artillery command became centralized, and supporting and defensive fires could be concentrated to best effect. The headlong pursuit by the Afrika Korps was brought to an abrupt halt by massed artillery fire, the position was firmly held, and after an interval for re-organization and re-supply, Montgomery began the famous battle of El Alamein, the start of the final upswing of British fortunes in the desert. There was still a great deal of fighting to be done by both the Eighth Army and the Anglo-American forces which landed in North Africa before the end came with the occupation of Tunis in the following year, but except for one or two aberrant engagements the artillery story throughout was one of text-book operation and efficiency.

Worthy of note as one of the aberrants is the action of 155 Field Battery RA at Sidi Nisr in Tunisia, on 26 February 1943. This battery, together with a battalion of the Hampshire Regiment, was deployed in a small position to act as a delaying force to cover the flank of the main British attack towards a feature known as 'Hunt's Gap' some twelve miles away. The small force was attacked by elements of the 10th Panzer Division, including a number of the relatively new Tiger tanks, and for the last time in the desert, and indeed in the war, the 25-pounders found themselves called upon to fight for their existence over open sights. In addition to the tank attacks the whole area was under heavy mortar fire for most of the day, plus frequent attacks by cannon-firing aircraft. The course of events can be summed up by extracts from a report based on the statements of survivors:

'By 1240 hrs enemy tanks, reported as thirty in number, and infantry had worked into positions around the flanks of the gun position. From captured maps it is also clear that self-propelled guns were being moved into positions at close range (600 yards). All this time the battery was engaging enemy infantry, machine guns, mortars etc., who were closing in on the Hampshire "B" and "D" company positions. Ammunition was being carried under extremely heavy fire along the road from Hampshire Farm to the gun position . . . At 1500 hrs a column of enemy infantry penetrated between Hampshire Farm and the gun position, and no more ammunition could pass. The enemy tanks in hull-down positions . . . engaged our guns one by one and set on fire ammunition dumps, killed the detachments and smashed the guns . . . "F" Troop was silenced by 1730 hrs. Tanks then moved down the road between "F" Troop and "E" Troop and surrounded "E" Troop. As it grew dark, at about 1830 hrs, Bren guns and at least one gun of "E" Troop were still in action against the enemy tanks at ranges of ten to twenty yards. The tanks smothered the gun position with machine gun and gun fire. Any man who moved was immediately shot . . . When the battle began there were 9 officers and 121 Other Ranks on the gun position . . . nine survived the action, of whom two are wounded and in hospital.'

Nine survivors from 130 men; proof that the German Army were a long way from being beaten and proof, if it were still needed, that isolated detachments of guns and infantry were a poor risk in the face of resolutely handled armour.

Chapter 3
THE TECHNICAL STRUGGLE

As the war progressed, so the need for improved artillery made itself felt; in field guns for greater range and shell-power, in anti-tank guns for greater penetrative ability, in anti-aircraft guns for higher ceiling and faster rates of fire. Confronted by this sort of demand there are two courses open to the designer; either to produce a completely new design of gun which provides the necessary improvement, or to make modifications to the existing model in order to work it to the extreme limits of efficiency and extract all the potential from it. In both cases he has a further alternative: either to achieve the improvement by orthodox ordnance engineering techniques or to seek an entirely new and unorthodox solution (bearing in mind that what is unorthodox today may well be routine practice tommorrow – if it succeeds).

In the matter of providing new designs, this was largely a case of producing more modern equivalents of weapons which were obsolescent when the war broke out, and in most cases the replacements had been on the drawing-boards well before 1939. One such example was the British 5.5-inch medium gun; the standard medium gun between the wars was the sixty-pounder, a five-inch calibre weapon which had first appeared in 1904. It had been improved in detail during the First World War, being given a better breech mechanism, a longer barrel and an improved carriage, the range going up in the process from 12,300 yards to 15,500 yards.

The sixty-pounder was supplemented by the 6-inch 26cwt howitzer, another First World War veteran which sent an 86lb shell to 11,400 yards, and before 1939 it was appreciated that both these weapons were past their prime. As with the smaller calibres the solution appeared to be a gun-howitzer, and a design of 5.5-inch gun-howitzer was drawn up, an equipment firing a 100lb shell to 16,200 yards, with a four-part charge to give flexibility in range coverage. Plans were approved in the spring of 1939 for production to begin in August, and the gun was formally approved for service on 31 August 1939. But the carriage design ran into difficulties, which in turn led to re-designs, delays and fresh trials, and it was not until late in 1941 that production finally began, and the new guns started to reach the troops in the spring of 1942.

Britain was also sadly deficient in heavy artillery, particularly after losing much of what existed in the fall of France. This was an area which had generated a good deal of debate in pre-war days since, as we have already seen, there was a body of opinion which held that the day of the long-range heavy guns was over, delivery of such weights of explosive at such ranges being the prerogative of the Royal Air Force. While this was, to some extent, true, the fact remained that aerial delivery could not yet be guaranteed on a 24-hour all-weather basis, as could gun delivery, and moreover it was apparent that the RAF were more engrossed in their potential role of war-winners by strategic bombing and not particularly inclined to exert themselves in the tactical army support role. In the end it became obvious that with all the will in the world the RAF were never going to be able to give the Army what it needed, since all its efforts were going into fighter defence and strategic bombing forces, and so in April 1938 the CIGS' Conference drew up specifications for a 6.85-inch gun firing a 100lb shell to 26,500 yards to replace the existing 6-inch heavy

The British 4.5-inch gun. This was part-nered by the 5.5-inch, on the same carriage, in Medium Regiments RA.

field gun, and a 7.85-inch howitzer to replace the existing 8-inch howitzer. These projects were examined from various angles, but in October 1939 they were both abandoned, the 6.85 completely and the 7.85 in favour of a re-design of the 9.2-inch howitzer.

The 9.2 had been designed in 1912-14, in the days when war was envisaged as a leisurely affair, and by the middle of 1940 the experiences in France had shown that it was far too cumbersome for modern warfare, while the 8-inch had insufficient range. An equipment capable of firing a 200lb shell to 15,500 yards was demanded, and since the re-design of the 9.2 called for in 1939 had hardly begun, the quickest solution was to take the existing 8-inch howitzer and re-line the barrel to 7.2 inches calibre to produce the 7.2-inch howitzer Mark 1. Approved in November 1940, the first equipments were produced in April 1941, but the stock of 8-inch howitzers available for re-building was limited, and in order to produce more 7.2s, numbers of 8-inch howitzers were bought from the United States and converted, becoming the 7.2-inch Marks 2, 3 or 4 depending upon which American model was used at the starting point for the conversion. In fact, although purchased from the U.S.A. these weapons were the same as the British models in most respects, having been built on contract in the U.S.A. during the First World War in order to outfit both the British Army and the American Expeditionary Force in France.

The performance of these conversions was rather better than had been

The 8-inch howitzer. These weapons had the barrels fitted with liners and the carriages fitted with pneumatic tyres to become the first 7.2-inch howitzers.

forecast, the maximum range being 16,900 yards, but the weapon itself was anachronistic. It used a two-wheeled box trail, as designed in 1915, but now fitted with enormous ballon-tyred wheels. The original 8-inch had fired a 200lb shell at 1,300ft/sec using a $9\frac{1}{4}$lb charge; the 7.2-inch conversion fired the same shell but at 1,700ft/sec by using a $19\frac{3}{4}$lb charge. As a result the recoil was considerably increased, beyond the amount which could be comfortably absorbed by the recoil system on the carriage, and when the howitzer was fired the whole equipment leapt backwards. To try and control this, huge wedges called 'quoins' were supplied, to be placed behind the carriage wheels so that upon recoil the wheels ran up the inclined surfaces of the quoins, absorbing the recoil momentum, and then ran down again to return the carriage to the firing position. The placing of the quoins was critical; too far behind the wheels and the weapon recoiled insufficiently far up the wedge and did not return to the correct place; too close, and the whole nine tons of howitzer and carriage charged up the ramp and sailed over the top, to fall behind with an earth-shaking crash.

In 1943 Britain received supplies of American 155mm guns and 8-inch Howitzers M1. These were 'partner pieces', mounted upon the same pattern of split-trail carriage, a modern and highly efficient design. The interchange of the 155mm gun (22ft 11 inches long and weighing 9,595 lb) and the 8-inch howitzer (17ft 6 inches long and weighing 10,240lb) was a relatively easy matter, demanding only changes in the arrangement of the supporting springs under the traversing roller race and adjustment of the pressures in the hydro-pneumatic recoil system and balancing presses, and it occurred to someone in Britain that if some extra carriages were acquired, then the 7.2-inch barrel could be mounted on to them and thus produce a far better weapon. Such a combination was, in fact, approved in November 1943 as the 7.2-inch howitzer Mark 5, but it is extremely doubtful if any, other than experimental models, were ever bulit; it was apparent that putting a converted 8-inch barrel on to modern mounting was the artillery equivalent of putting old wine into new bottles, and a far better solution would be to produce a completely new 7.2-inch barrel with a better ballistic performance. A new model, with a 20ft 8-inch barrel was rapidly produced and approved in December 1943 as the Mark 6, and this, on the American mounting, was so stable that an additional propelling charge was developed to give the 200lb shell a maximum range of 19,600 yards.

Meanwhile the new design of 9.2-inch howitzer had reached the prototype stage. This used a split-trail carriage which appeared to have been heavily influenced by the American 155mm 8-inch design, having a similar four-wheeled bogie at the front and the split trail ends carried on a two-wheeled limber. This weapon fired a 315lb shell to 16,000 yards, not a very good performance considering the equivalent German weapon, the 24cm Haubitze 39, fired a 365lb shell to 19,700 yards, and in

The 7.2-inch
howitzer Mark 6 on
the American
155mm carriage, an
amalgamation
which permitted an
increase in range
from 16,900 yards to
19,600.

The experimental
9.2-inch howitzer of
1941-42, a cumber-
some equipment
which promised but
a poor improve-
ment on the earlier
model, although it
was easier to
emplace.

The American
240mm howitzer, a
design of classic
simplicity and great
effectiveness. Its
availability in 1942
ended super-heavy
gun development in
Britain for all time.

The 240mm
howitzer carriage
would also accept
the barrel of the 8-
inch Gun M1. Both
equipments
travelled in two
units, carriage and
barrel, on transport
wagons. Here the 8-
inch barrel is about
to be lifted from its
wagon to be lowered
on to the emplaced
carriage behind the
crane.

October 1942 'consideration of the adoption of this equipment was held
in abeyance', a polite way of saying 'let's see if anything better turns up.'
Fortunately, something did – indeed, it might well be that this was the
factor which led to the 'abeyance' decision – when the U.S. Army
standardized two new equipments in 1942, the 240mm howitzer M1 and
its partner piece the 8-inch Gun M1. These, like the 155mm gun and 8-
inch howitzer combination, shared a common design of mounting, a
split-trail pattern of ingenious and excellent design. For transport the
mounting and gun were separated and hoisted on to transport wagons

by a 20-ton crane which formed part of the gun battery. In default of the crane the design allowed the weapons to be dismantled or put together by using the power winches on the towing tractors, though this method took more time. The 240mm fired a 360lb shell to 25,225 yards, better than anything else of this calibre had ever done, while the 8-inch gun fired a 240lb shell to 35,365 yards. With weapons of this class available, the 9.2-inch was abandoned completely.

In the case of German development there was generally some more specific aim in view than a general all-round improvement. An example of their approach can be seen in the gradual improvement of their standard 105mm field howitzer, the Model 18. This had been designed by Rheinmettal and entered service in 1935 to become the standard

The carriage of the 240mm howitzer after lowering to the ground over a pre-pared pit. The hoisting slings are being removed, while a gunner in the pit prepares the recoil spade attach-ment. At the left can be seen one of the jack feet of the crane, and in the rear is the 38-ton M6 tractor, one of which towed each unit of the gun.

The 105mm leFH 18, standard field howitzer of the German Army throughout the war.

divisional field-piece. It was an orthodox split-trail, two-wheeled carriage equipment firing a 32.6lb shell to 11,675 yards and weighing 4,865lb in action. While this was satisfactory in most respects, the most fervent supporter had to admit that the maximum range was poor in comparison with the British 25-pounder (13,400 yards) and the Soviet 76.2mm M1939. Admittedly, the 105mm Model 18 threw a heavier shell, but to the recipient the difference between a 25lb shell and a 32lb shell was largely academic; range was the big thing, once battle was joined.

Accordingly, in 1940 the performance was improved by fitting a muzzle brake, increasing the pressure in the recoil system, and providing a new and more powerful cartridge and a long-range shell of better aero-dynamic shape. With this combination the range went up to 13,500 yards, which was held to be sufficient, and the new weapon was known as the Model 18M.

Next came a familiar cry from the troops, a request to reduce the weight while retaining the performance. This request was made in March 1942 after experience in manhandling guns during the Russian winter, and the designers did their best to provide a quick answer by taking the carriage of the 75mm PAK 40 anti-tank gun, which was in volume production, making a few modifications, and attaching the gun and recoil system of the model 18M on top, calling the result the Model 18/40. While this seemed sound enough on paper, when all the necessary modifications had been done the total weight came out at only 65lb less than the original Model 18, which wasn't a lot to show for all the work. However, since the carriage was somewhat easier to make than the original design had been, and since production of one pattern of carriage for two guns was economic sense, the Model 18/40 was accepted as an interim measure, while the designers went back to try again.

They re-appeared with a design called the Model 42, which mounted the 18M barrel and breech in a completely new split-trail carriage with wide track and tubular trail legs. This brought the weight down to 3,580 lb, a reduction of 785lb, and an improved recoil system permitted an increase in the propelling charge to give a maximum range of 14,200 yards. Unfortunately for the designers, while this weapon had been in the design stage the Army had been doing some fundamental re-assessment of the role and requirements of field artillery in the light of their experience in Russia, and they now issued a specification which made some new features mandatory in any future design and which put the Model 42 on the scrap heap before it got past the prototype stage. The first demand was that the weapon had to fire at angles over 45°; this meant that it had to elevate from zero to 45°, covering all the ranges from the muzzle to the maximum, and then continue to elevate and shoot so that as the elevation increased, so the range decreased. In this way every range would be reached by two elevations, one below 45° and one above, so that the weapon could use direct fire or howitzer-like plunging fire.

Next came a demand for a maximum range of 14,200 yards (13 Km) without requiring special charges or long-range shells. Then the weapon had to have a mounting which allowed it to traverse through 360° and fire at any angle of traverse, a feature now considered vital in situations where the artillery was in a position encircled by an enemy and likely to have to fire in any direction. And lastly it had to weigh no more than the Model 18M (4,265lb) and be equally manoeuvrable.

This was a stiff specification, and one can scarely blame the Rheinmettal-Borsig company for declining to compete. But Krupp and Skoda both made the attempt, using a barrel and breech based on a common ballistic solution but going their own ways with the carriage designs.

The Skoda design was basically a normal split-trail, two-wheeled carriage to which a firing support pedestal, under the axle, and two more trail legs, under the barrel, were added. In action the gun rested on the central pedestal, its wheels off the ground, with the four trail legs swung out to form outriggers. Spades were driven in at the trail ends, making an extremely stable platform on which the gun could traverse and shoot through 360°. A most ingenious feature was a hydraulic system on the trail legs which did away with the need to find or level a large flat space. The legs were permitted to lie at whatever level the

The Skoda 105mm howitzer leFH 43, showing the four-legged support and firing pedestal when in action.

ground allowed; the hydraulic system allowed slow movement of the trail legs about their hinges, such as when folding or unfolding the legs when coming into or going out of action. But a sudden movement of the legs due to the firing shock was resisted by sensitive valves which prevented movement of the liquid in the system and effectively locked the legs at whatever angle they lay.

The whole equipment weighed 4,840lb, slightly over the specified limit, and the maximum range with the standard 32.6lb shell was 16,400 yards.

The Krupp company produced two designs, one using a three-legged mounting very similar to the Skoda type and weighing 5,275lb, and the other using a cruciform four-wheeled mounting very similar to the sort of mounting produced for anti-aircraft guns but with a much lower silhouette. Most of the components for this came from the in-production 88mm PAK 43 anti-tank gun, which was a good economy move, but at 5,400lb it was well over the weight limit.

But time had run out on the 105mm howitzer. Before the designs of the Model 43, as the new design was called, were finalised, the war ended. Undoubtedly the Skoda design was the better, and even today it is still held up to would-be designers as an example. But the Krupp design using in-production components would probably have stood a better chance of being adopted on economic grounds in spite of its excess weight. It is worth noting that similar designs of carriage for a 15cm gun were prepared by Skoda, and since the end of the war both the French and the Russians have produced weapons which seem to owe a lot of their inspiration to the Skoda designs.

In the United States development was on a vastly different footing. This was largely due to the fortunate fact that the designs worked on during the 1930s all came to fruition in 1940/41, and except for the opening months of the war, when production was getting into its stride, the U.S. Army was equipped with modern weapons across the entire range and was less in need of fresh designs. As a result the development programme was more detailed, searching for answers to specific problems or simply advancing the knowledge of ballistics so that the next generation of ordnance would have a sound technical foundation from which to build. A notable feature of the American effort was its size; innumerable variants of guns and carriages would be produced by the wide variety of design agencies and private companies in order to examine some likely avenues of research. If an idea succeeded, it was followed up; if it didn't, it was discarded; while this resembles the German approach in some respects, it differs in the basic fact that the Americans could afford this diverse approach since it did not interfere with production of standard weapons for the Army's immediate use.

A good example of the American system can be seen by examining some of the projects revolving around one gun, the 90mm anti-aircraft

gun. The 90mm M1 was the father of the tribe; this was a sound design of anti-aircraft gun on a two-wheeled cruciform carriage, firing a 23.4lb shell at 2,700ft/sec to a maximum ceiling of 32,000 feet at a rate of 15 rounds a minute. Designed in the mid-1930s, it was rushed into service in 1940, and 2,000 guns were in the hands of troops by the time of the North African landings in late 1942. It was then followed by the M2 design which incorporated a mechanical fuze-setter-and-rammer to increase the rate of fire, and had the carriage re-designed to allow the gun to be fired from its wheels in an emergency; its ballistic performance was the same as the M1.

The American 90mm anti-aircraft Gun M2, an improvement on the original model in that the design catered for such diverse requirements as anti-tank and anti-torpedo-boat firing.

Trials showed that, like most anti-aircraft guns, the 90mm had a useful anti-tank potential, penetrating 109mm at 1,000 yards with a simple piercing shell. As a result of this discovery the M3 gun was developed, little more than an M1 modified to go into tank or self-propelled mountings. A tungsten-cored shot was developed which could defeat 173mm of plate at 1,000 yards.

These were the three 90mm guns which were standardized and issued during the war. But now let us run briefly through the more significant variations of the 90mm built for development purposes. The anti-aircraft line began with the M1A1E1, an M1 using liquid injection cooling in an attempt to increase bore life by reducing flame temperature and thus erosive wear, while the M1A1E2 had the chamber modified to take ammunition fitted with the 'Fisa Protector', a hardened steel sleeve at the cartridge mouth intended to protect the throat of the gun chamber from erosion by hot gases. The 90mm T5 had the barrel rifled on the 'Probert' system used in the British 3.7-inch Mark 6 anti-aircraft gun in which the depth of the rifling grooves gradually reduced, until the last few inches of the gun barrel were smooth-bored. The shell was fitted with a special driving band and centering bands at the shoulder, and the whole design was an attempt to develop higher velocity, reduce wear, and eject the shell from the muzzle with the best possible ballistic shape.

The 90mm Gun T6 used the same ammunition as the T5 but in a normally-rifled barrel as a comparison. The T16 had a barrel 70 calibres long, six feet longer than the M1, and was an attempt to produce a hyper-velocity gun pushing the shell out at 3,500ft/sec; the T16E1 was T16 using Fisa Protectors, while the T16E2 had a chrome-plated bore and used shells on which the driving band was pre-cut to suit the rifling. The T19 was an M1 with a 'Crane Liner', a specially-hardened alloy lining inside the chamber and the first 64 inches of rifling, another attempt at decreasing the rate of wear.

In the tank gun field the M3 led firstly to the M3E2, with chrome-plated bore. Then came the T15E1, E2 and E3, attempts to produce a

One of the better Japanese anti-aircraft guns was actually a 'redistributed' Naval gun, the 8cm Model 3, with an effective ceiling of 17,000 feet. An unusual detail was the canting of the breech to the left in order to make loading easier.

better penetration figure; the T15E2 used separate-loading ammunition and was approved for standardization in June 1945 but the project was stopped shortly afterwards since nobody had ordered any tanks into which to fit the guns. The T54 was a short-chambered T15E2 with a barrel 70 calibres long, firing tungsten-cored shot at 3,750ft/sec to penetrate 300mm of armour at 1,000 yards, a development which continued after the war.

Since the piercing performance, even of the basic guns, was so good, it is not surprising to find the 90mm being put forward as a possible towed anti-tank gun. The basic model in this group was the Gun T8 on Carriage T5E2, an extremely good design combination. The gun was little more than the basic M1, while the carriage was a conventional two-wheeled, split-trail type with a shield and a caster wheel on the trail ends to assist manhandling. This fired tungsten-cored shot at 3,350ft/sec, defeating 250mm at 1,000 yards, but the design was eventually turned down since it was too heavy at 7,000lb. The next attempt was the T13 gun on T9 carriage, a somewhat unconventional design in which the

The American 90mm Gun T13, an interesting and unusual anti-tank equipment. In this picture the trail legs are being folded forward from the firing to the travelling position.

The 90mm T13 with the trail legs folded for travelling. Notice the efficient muzzle brake, heavy breech ring, and the firing pedestal folded beneath the axle. A brilliant piece of engineering but already beginning to show the creeping penalty of high velocity anti-tank gun design — it weighed almost four tons.

shield became a structural member and the trail legs, hinged to the top corners of the shield, swung round to lie under the barrel for travelling. Ballistically the T13 gun was the same as the M3, and though the design was commended and the weapon fired successful trials, manufacture was not recommended since a 3-inch gun development promised similar performance and less weight. Other anti-tank developments were the T18 and T21 guns, using different chamber capacities to achieve 3,500 ft/sec and 3,150ft/sec respectively; the T20, an improved T8; and the T22, a 90mm gun with a 105mm AA gun chamber and firing the 105mm cartridge to produce high velocity. Other anti-tank carriage designs included the T9E2, capable of being dismantled into eight loads for air transport and yet be re-assembled in 15 seconds – which sounds a trifle optimistic to me.

Obviously, consideration of the T-model numbers shows that many designs have not been mentioned, and a similar run-down could be done on many other weapons. The 3-inch anti-aircraft gun, for example, was at the T-63 stage when the war ended, while the 105mm anti-aircraft gun got up to T-32.

Consideration of some of these trials designs, however, indicates that we are moving away from straightforward developmental improvement into the realms of specific feature improvement, and in order to explore this area more thoroughly we need to know just what the designer is trying to do and how he proposes to do it. The most basic thing to understand about gun improvement is that the easiest way to improve a gun is to leave it alone and improve the ammunition, a process which is generally quicker, always cheaper, and usually produces more improvement for a given amount of effort than does fiddling with gun design. (This, of course, is said in the assumption that the gun in question is a good basic design to begin with; no amount of tinkering with the ammunition can do much to help a badly designed gun.)

A gun's performance, in any role, revolves round the muzzle velocity it imparts to the projectile; whether the desired end is to penetrate some more armour, reach higher into the sky or reach further across land or sea, the one thing which will achieve it is an increase in velocity, and the ways of attaining this increase are fairly well defined. The first, and obvious, method is to increase the propelling charge; in round figures, a four-fold increase in the size of the charge will give an increase of some 60 per cent in velocity. Such a simple statement is bound to have a catch in it, and this one has several; the gun needs to be strengthened to withstand the increase in pressure, the chamber has to be enlarged to accept the larger charge, the recoil system will have to be modified to take the additional thrust, the consumption of propellant brings production problems, and the erosive wear of the gun barrel would be horrible to contemplate.

The second simple solution is to increase the length of the gun barrel so that the projectile is exposed to the accelerating effect of the cartridge explosion for a longer time. In order to obtain the same 60 per cent increase in velocity the barrel would have to be increased to three times its former length, a proposition which again is scarcely practical.

Thirdly one can compromise between these two solutions, making the charge larger and the barrel longer; our 60 per cent increase in muzzle velocity would now be reached with a 50 per cent increase in charge weight and a 50 per cent increase in barrel length, and again, neither of these can be considered as practical measures. The only consolation to be found when contemplating these three methods is that increases in the order of our theoretical 60 per cent are rarely demanded; most users would be satisfied with a 10 per cent improvement, and such a degree calls for less drastic measures.

Finally, leaving the gun and cartridge alone, velocity can be increased by lightening the projectile. Halving the projectile weight will increase velocity by about 40 per cent, a very attractive solution but one which still carries a built-in disadvantage: by lightening the projectile we upset the 'ballistic coefficient', that property of a projectile best described as its 'carrying power' and which is closely related to the ratio of weight to diameter. Too little weight for a given diameter and the carrying power is reduced, leading to a rapid fall-off in velocity after leaving the muzzle. It is this property which leads to the anomalous performance of lightweight full-calibre tungsten-cored piercing shot; its muzzle velocity is high, due to its light weight, and its performance at short ranges impressive. But as the range increases, so the lack of 'carrying power' tells, causing loss of velocity until at, say, 1,200 yards, the striking velocity is lower than that of a conventional full-weight steel shot and so the penetrative performance is worse. The steel shot started off with less velocity at the muzzle, but due to its better weight-diameter ratio retained its velocity better during flight.

Another obstacle to developing high velocity weapons lies in the need to provide the shell with a driving band of soft metal which will bite into the rifling so as to spin the shell and also act as a seal to keep the propelling gases behind the shell and pushing it out of the gun. The enormous radial stress generated as the shell bites into the rifling and is forced both forward and into rotation places an enormous stress on the driving band, and attempts to push the shell faster lead to the copper driving band shearing and the shell failing to spin at all.

A solution to this was first explored by the Germans in their Paris Gun of the First World War. Firing at a velocity of 5,900ft/sec with a 264 lb 21cm shell, no combination of copper driving band and conventional multi-grooved rifling could survive the initial acceleration, and the solution adopted was to rifle the gun with a small number of deep grooves and build spiral ribs on the wall of the shell to match them.

Thus the shell was a mechanical fit in the rifling, the stress was distributed over a greater area, and a sealing band of copper and asbestos was hand-loaded behind the shell in order to provide the gas seal.

The same solution was adopted in 1935 when the German Army demanded a new supergun, the 21cm Kanone 12(E). (12 since 12 × 10 kilometres was the estimated range; (E) for Eisenbahnlafette, or railway mounting.) An eight-groove barrel was developed, with ribbed shells to suit, and with a 530lb charge it fired a 236lb shell at 4,920ft/sec to reach a maximum range of 71.4 miles. Two of these superguns were built, differing in the construction of their mountings, and in 1940 they were deployed on the French coast to fire into south-eastern England. Fragments of the unmistakeable shells were picked up at Rainham, near

The German K12(E) super-gun launches a shell at Kent in 1941.

Ribbed shells for the German 21cm K12(E) long-range gun. The raised ribs engaged with corresponding grooves in the gun barrel in order to spin the shell at the high velocity demanded.

Chatham, about 55 miles from the nearest point on French soil. These two guns, built at considerable expense (one and a half million marks apiece is the generally accepted figure) seem not to have made any other contribution to the war; their barrel life was of the order of 120 shots before erosion from the massive charge so wore away the rifling that the shell could no longer be relied upon to align itself accurately. An interesting assessment was made by the Ordnance Board of the economic viability of this gun; assuming that all the 120 shells were aimed at the same spot, and allowing for the dispersion to be expected at the maximum range of the gun, the net result would be the distribution of 1,920lb of high explosive over an area of about 100 acres; one pound of explosive for every 252 square yards.

Even so, even with this sort of arithmetic being bandied about and appreciated, the British manufactured a similar weapon. The idea first appeared in March 1940 as a more-or-less idle enquiry by the Ordnance Board of the Director of Artillery as to whether he had any hyper-velocity weapons in mind. His reply was fairly definite: 'No such requirement has yet been put to us, nor do we intend to suggest the idea ... Even if it should be possible to build a gun of reasonable life and sufficient accuracy ... the limitations imposed on the size and capacity of the projectiles raise considerable doubts as to whether the labour involved would produce results comparable with aircraft bombing. . .'

However, a splined-barrel hyper-velocity gun is a very useful experimental and research tool to have, if you can persuade somebody to buy you one; a difficult task in peacetime, but much easier in war. So there was little opposition when the Director of Naval Ordnance raised the question again in 1942. The first proposal was to make an 8-inch 140-calibre (8″×140=93ft 4-inch) barrel; the principal drawback to that was that the largest gun-lathes in the country were built to take the 62-foot Naval 16-inch gun and they could take nothing longer. A suggestion was made to produce the barrel in two parts and screw them together in the centre, but on mature consideration, this idea was turned down. Shortly afterwards the DNO suggested inserting an 8-inch calibre liner of the maximum possible length (60 feet) into a 13.5-inch calibre bored-out barrel, using the 13.5-inch propelling charge to fire a ribbed 256lb shell. This was agreed to, and by the end of 1942 the gun had been built, installed on a proof mounting on the Isle of Grain, and fired. Since the site did not allow the maximum range to be developed – the gun was being fired northward so that the flight of the shell and its descent could be observed from the Shoeburyness gunnery ranges – a second equipment was sent to Dover and emplaced in the Royal Marine Siege Battery near St Margaret's Bay, where for some reason or other it acquired the nickname 'Bruce' – probably after Admiral of the Fleet Sir Bruce Fraser, then Controller of the Navy. 'Bruce' was fired from Dover in March 1943 and at various times thereafter, producing a good deal of information about the behaviour of shells and fuzes at high velocities and altitude. The muzzle velocity was 4,600ft/sec and the maximum range achieved was 170,000 yards (62½ miles), but the accurate life of the gun was no more than thirty rounds due to the enormous erosive effect of the 147lb cordite charge. Various suggestions were made for modifications which would reduce the wear, but eventually the project was closed down.

The Germans, during all this time, had been taking a fresh look at the driving band problem; the ribbed shell was obviously only suitable for extremely long-range guns where expense was of little moment, and something more simple was needed for guns likely to fire large quantities of ammunition. After trials with various metals they finally developed a band made from sintered iron which was far more resistant to shear than was the conventional copper band, allowing high velocities, and which was much more economical in that it did not use such a scarce and costly material as copper. The first applications in service showed the drawback that it wore out gun barrels by frictional abrasion much faster than did copper, but this was overcome by changing the twist of rifling and the extensive adoption of increasing twist in which the degree of radial acceleration was low to begin with and increased in proportion to the shell's increase in forward velocity as it neared the gun's muzzle.

With the possibilities of increased performance from charge, barrel length and driving band design thoroughly explored, it becomes necessary to begin looking at more unorthodox solutions. The taper bore, already mentioned, was one field which the German technicians examined very thoroughly and brought into service to good effect. Unfortunately its prime use, in anti-tank guns, was allied to the use of tungsten-cored ammunition, since this allowed collapsible steel skirts to be fitted around the core and, since these light steel skirts collapsed to a small emergent diameter, the ballistic coefficient of the shot was good, leading to good penetrative performance at longer ranges. The unfortunate aspect of this was the scarcity of tungsten in Germany, which became so acute that after 1943 it was entirely reserved for machine tool production and the use of taper-bore anti-tank guns therefore ceased when their supply of ammunition dried up.

But as the taper bore declined, so an alternative system arose, the coned bore. This may at first sight appear to be little more than a matter of semantics, but the distinction is that in a taper bore the whole gun barrel is evenly tapered from breech to muzzle: in a coned bore the gun barrel is of the normal parallel form for most of its length, having a short 'squeeze section' either as part of the barrel assembly or added to the gun muzzle as a screw-on attachment. The projectile attains normal velocity in the parallel section of the barrel and is then subjected to a sudden squeeze and boost in velocity as it passes through the coned section. The

first, and the only service, application of the squeeze adapter was on the British two-pounder with 'Littlejohn Adapter', used on the two-pounder gun in armoured cars and tanks. This device was proposed by a Mr Janacek in July 1940, but it was turned down, partly on the grounds that it seemed unlikely to work, but principally because the need to modify guns and set up new production capacity for the special projectiles could not be countenanced at the difficult time. In March 1941 the idea was put forward once more, and this time a development contract was approved and work on the adapter and ammunition began as a relatively low priority. In August of that year a German 28/20mm taper-bore gun and ammunition was captured in Cyrenacia, and the revelation that such a weapon was actually is use was enough to speed the Janacek project. Eventually, late in 1942, the adapters were issued, together with the tungsten-cored collapsing-skirt projectiles, but by that time the six-pounder gun was beginning to replace the two-pounder and the 'Littlejohn' system saw relatively little use.

In Germany the use of adapters was pioneered by Rheinmettal-Borsig, whose Dr Banck became the foremost expert on the subject. The application of adapters was proposed for anti-aircraft guns, in order to increase velocity, reduce the time of flight and so improve the chance of hitting; and for heavy artillery in order to achieve greater range. Banck's eventual solution was to produce a shell of a calibre capable of passing through the squeeze and then build it up to the full calibre by 'collapsing bolts' on the shell shoulder and a collapsing skirt driving band at the shell's base. The collapsing bolts were of soft metal, hollow, and shaped as truncated cones; three such bolts equi-spaced around the shell centred it in the bore but were easily squeezed down during their

The schweres Panzerbuchse 41, a taper-bore gun with a chamber calibre of 28mm and an emergent calibre of 21mm. Shown here during its test at Pendine, South Wales, in 1941 which revealed a velocity of 4,590 feet a second and spurred on British research in this field.

A collapsing bolt shell for a 105mm anti-aircraft gun with squeezebore attachment on the muzzle. On passing through the squeeze the bolts were forced into recess in the shell body while the skirt band was pressed backwards.

passage through the adapter. The rear skirt, of sintered iron, was radially compressed to the rear to form an extension of the shell body contour so that the end result was a shell free of excrescences and with good ballistic properties.

In general terms it was held that the use of a squeeze adapter could be expected to increase velocity and maximum range by about 30 per cent, and in the anti-aircraft application it was hoped to develop service muzzle velocities in the 1,150-1,200 metres per second (3,775-3,950ft/sec) area. Adapters were developed for the 88mm Flak 18, emergent calibre 70mm, velocity 3,900ft/sec; for the 88mm Flak 41, emergent calibre 70mm, velocity 4,500ft/sec; for the 105mm Flak 39, emergent calibre 88mm, velocity 3,700ft/sec; and for the 128mm Flak 40, emergent calibre 105mm, velocity 3,650ft/sec. However, none of these equipments was sufficiently perfected to enter service before the war ended. Numerous projects were also under examination for increasing the range of heavy artillery; the most advanced of these was the work on the 24cm Kanone Model 3 a 24/21cm squeeze design promising 3,600ft/sec with 185lb shell to give a range of 54,700 (31 miles) an increase of 13,000 yards on the performance of the standard gun, an increase of 32 per cent which more or less supports the rule of thumb given above.

Attempts to improve performance by using a lighter projectile are, as we have already seen, foredoomed to failure in view of the ballistic coefficient problem. But the theory of the squeeze bore gives an indication of a way around the problem; if the projectile can be arranged so that it is a full-calibre lightweight inside the gun barrel but a small calibre heavyweight outside the muzzle, one can have the best of both worlds. The way to achieve this had been pioneered by a French ordnance engineer, Edgar Brandt, in the 1930s with his 'discarding sabot projectile'. In this system a 'sub-projectile' of smaller calibre than the parent gun was fitted into a 'sabot' or sleeve of light metal construction which brought the overall calibre up to that of the gun. Thus the projectile when in the gun was of less weight than a conventional projectile of the same calibre, due to the large amount of light metal and air spacing

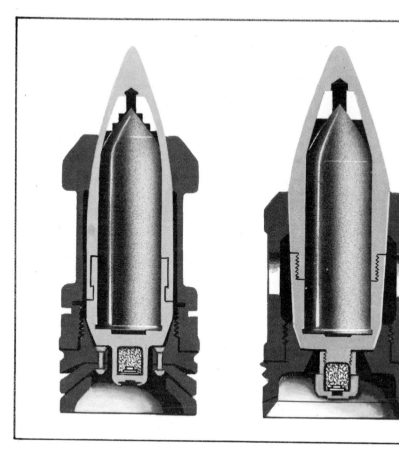

A discarding sabot projectile in section. The central portion is the tungsten carbide core sheathed in steel to form the sub-projectile. The remainder is of light alloy, weakened so as to break apart on firing and be discarded when it leaves the gun muzzle.

A selection of anti-tank projectiles, illustrating their development. On the left a standard steel shot with piercing and ballistic caps; centre a German composite rigid shot with tungsten core and lightweight body; on the right a British six-pounder discarding sabot shot whole and sectioned.

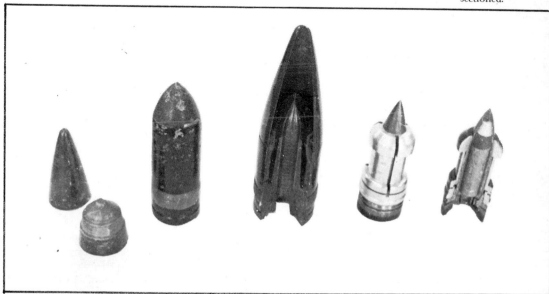

in the sabot, and when fired it reached a high velocity. The sabot was so designed that upon leaving the muzzle it broke up into a number of pieces and fell away from the sub-projectile. Since this, devoid of the sabot, had a better weight/diameter ratio, its ballistic coefficient was good and so it retained its velocity to considerable ranges. There were other attractions in this system; the gun required no adapters or modifications, so it could use conventional ammunition when the high velocity performance was not needed; the lightweight sabot projectile could use a more powerful propelling charge, giving an even greater increase in velocity; and the ammunition promised to be relatively simple, since standard manufactured projectiles of a suitably smaller calibre could be utilised as the sub-projectiles.

Both Britain and Germany were attracted by Brandt's idea, but their application of it moved in different directions. British work was aimed almost exclusively at producing a high-velocity anti-tank piercing projectile, and for this purpose the sub-projectile was a tungsten carbide core in a steel sheath, with a sabot of light alloy which split into four pieces and discarded shortly after clearing the muzzle. Work on this design began in 1940 using a 25mm Hotchkiss anti-tank gun as the vehicle. Once this had shown the feasibility of the idea, sabot shot was developed for the 6-pounder and 17-pounder guns, entering service in 1944. It provided the gun with a startling increase in performance; the 17-pounder gun's steel shot penetration was 110mm at 1,000 yards, and the discarding sabot projectile increased this to 231mm.

In Germany, due to the tungsten supply problem, this side of sabot design was not explored. Instead, anti-tank projectiles used the next smaller calibre of issue piercing shell as their sub-projectile; in spite of this handicap, the results achieved were quite worthwhile, which as much as anything reflects the superlative design and construction of German piercing shells. For example the 105mm field howitzer Model 18/40 fired a normal 34.6lb piercing shell at 1,275ft/sec to defeat 62mm of plate at 1,000 yards; the sabot projectile, Panzergranate 39TS, was based on the 88mm gun piercing shell inside a sabot, weighed 17lb and produced a velocity of 2,520ft/sec to defeat 80mm at the same range, a 28 per cent increase. These may not be very spectacular figures when compared with the specialist anti-tank guns, but for a field howitzer they were quite respectable.

Much more work went into the development of sabot shells for increasing the range of high explosive projectiles, and in this application advantage was taken of the sabot principle to try and produce a better ballistic shape in the sub-projectile. The 'normal' artillery shell is an uneasy compromise between the best aerodynamic shape and the most practical shape for travelling up the gun barrel. In flight the ideal shape would be a cigar-like article with tapering nose and tail and scarcely any parallel section in the middle, but in order to obtain stability inside the barrel it is necessary to give the shell a long parallel-walled body to provide a bearing surface. When bore stability is being attended to by the sabot, the designer can take the opportunity to make the sub-projectile to a shape more closely approaching the ideal, though he is still under some restraint due to the practical necessity of putting a worth-while payload into the shell and fitting some sort of fuzing system to it, both of which may conflict with his ideal shape.

The German experimenters explored every conceivable variant of the basic sabot principle; semi-sabot shells, full calibre at the shoulder and tapering into a sub-calibre base supported by a sabot; full-calibre at the base with sub-calibre shoulders supported by sabots; sub-calibre shells with pot-like sabots which discarded axially in one unit; shells with base and shoulder sabots connected by a cage, so that the discard of the shoulder sections was radial and that of the base section axial; sub-calibre shells with unconnected shoulder and base sabots which discarded independently; all these and many others were tried. Much of the work was applied to anti-aircraft guns in order to increase velocity; the 88mm Flak 41 had a 70mm sub-projectile achieving 4,200ft/sec and the 128mm Flak 40 a 105mm sub-projectile giving 3,650ft/sec. Designs for long-range firing from medium and heavy guns were also explored. But very few of these designs reached the firing stage and few shells were produced in sufficient numbers to be placed in even limited service with troops. This is difficult to understand, since both Britain and Germany began more or less at the same time and at the same level of knowledge, yet the British had discarding sabot ammunition in service a year before the war ended. It was probably the multiplicity of German designs which was resposible for their slow development; as in many other fields of wartime research, far too many projects were being pursued at the same time. Had the effort been concentrated into a smaller number of projects more thoroughly and systematically investigated, a more practical result might have been achieved.

In view of the difficulties raised by the problems of rifling and driving bands, it will be no surprise to find that the possibility of dispensing with rifling and reverting to smooth-bore ordnance was actively considered. In Britain it never amounted to much; the principal suggestions were for a number of smooth-bore taper-bore guns, largely for pure research and with little expectation of producing a service weapon. One or two were built and fired to produce valuable research data and that was that. In Germany, though, the availablity of the Peenemunde Research Establishment and various other research centres, amply provided with wind tunnels and other aids to aerodynamic experiments, led to much exploration into fin-stabilised projectiles which culminated in the production of the Peenemunde Arrow Shell, a remarkable projectile by any standards.

It is not at all certain whether the Arrow Shell came first and went

The Peenemunde Arrow Shell developed for the 31cm smooth-bored railway gun. The body is 12cm calibre and 75 inches long, while the fins and driving ring are of 31cm calibre. It achieved a range in excess of 93 miles on trial.

looking for a suitable gun, or whether the gun designers went looking for a suitable projectile, but the most spectacular application of the Arrow Shell, and the only one to see actual use in combat, was its development as a super-long-range shell for the 28cm Kanone 5 (E) railway gun. This was a 215-ton weapon which normally fired a 563lb ribbed shell from a 12-grooved barrel to a maximum range of 68,000 yards (38.6 miles). Various expedients for increasing range were suggested, and eventually its maximum performance was reached by smooth-boring the barrel to 31cm calibre and providing an arrow shell. This shell was a 12cm calibre, 6ft 3inch long dart, with four 31cm calibre fins at its rear end and a 31cm discarding sabot support ring at its mid-point. Since the all-up weight was only 300lb, and since the absence of rifling lowered the resistance to movement in the barrel, it was possible to increase the propelling charge, and instead of the normal 380lb charge, the arrow shell was launched by a 550lb cartridge. It left the barrel at 5,000ft/sec and produced a maximum range during trials of 151,000 yards – 93.83 miles. What nobody has ever produced is a reliable figure for the accuracy to be expected at that range. Two guns were fitted with the smooth bore barrel and one was used to bombard the U.S. Third Army in the latter days of the war, at a range estimated at 70 miles.

Arrow shells were also developed for the 105mm Flak 39 anti-aircraft gun; numerous designs, differing in minor features, were tried and a velocity of 3,125ft/sec was claimed. But the use of arrow shells in this role was complicated by the supply problem; while a long-range gun such as the 31cm would be satisfied with firing half a dozen shots a day, an anti-aircraft gun, to be credible, needed a rate of fire of 15-20 rounds a minute. Arrow shells demanded precise manufacture from high-quality steel, a demand impossible of realisation by the time the designs had been perfected, and so sconomics once more called a halt to a promising development. It might be worth adding that a fin-stabilised discarding sabot projectile, owing much to the Peenemunde Arrow Shell, was to be the standard projectile for the last British heavy anti-aircraft gun, the 5

inch 'Green Mace' of the 1950s, the development of which was over-taken by the perfection of guided missiles; that the Soviets now use a similar projectile in their 115mm smooth-bore tank gun; and that there are rumours of an arrow shell revival for a new German heavy gun in the mid-1970s.

One last area to be investigated was the possibility of improving the shell's performance after it had left the muzzle by turning it into a self-propelled missile. Since the rocket was a weapon held to be of considerable promise by the Germans (although, strangely, they made less use of it tactically than did any of the Allied nations) it is not surprising that the application of rocket boost to artillery shells was investigated. The first attempts were simple; the rear end of the shell was appropriated for the installation of a solid-fuel rocket motor venting through a hole in the shell base. A pyrotechnic delay unit in the rocket vent was ignited by the cartridge explosion in the gun chamber, and as the shell approached its vertex (the highest point of the trajectory) the delay burned through and ignited the rocket motor which then delivered thrust to boost the shell's failing speed and thus increase the range.

This worked well enough, but the additional boost pushed up the terminal velocity and the shells tended to land very hard, burying their noses deep into the ground before the fuze could detonate the payload, thus smothering the detonation and reducing the shell's effect. A second type of shell was then developed in which the motor was in the nose section, venting through ports arranged around the shell shoulder, and with the payload at the rear end. This cured the smothering problem but the rush of hot gas over the shell body upset the airflow and the shell was wildly inaccurate. Finally came a compromise, with the rocket motor in the nose of the shell, the payload at the rear, and the rocket blast conducted down a central pipe, through the explosive compartment (which posed some pretty problems about insulation) to vent through the rear of the shell. This model solved all the problems.

But it was an expensive and difficult item to manufacture and it was never taken into service in great numbers. The only weapon to use rocket-assisted shells in quantity was the 28cm Kanone 5 (E) railway gun, which adopted one as an intermediate stage between its normal shell and the Peenemunde Arrow Shell. This 547lb shell used a 45lb solid-fuel rocket motor and achieved a range of 94,600 yards (53.75 miles) which was very impressive. Less impressive was the accuracy; at that range only 50 per cent of the shots fired fell into a rectangle 3.4 kilometres long by 250 metres wide.

Theoretically the rocket shell was an inefficient device, since it needed to carry such a quantity of rocket propellant that the amount of payload remaining was insufficient – the 28cm shell only carried 31lb of high explosive, $5\frac{1}{2}$ per cent of its total weight. A Dr Tromsdroff proposed to improve matters with his 'Athodyd' shell, which was to all intents a flying ramjet motor surrounded by explosive. He theorised that it was wasteful to carry propellant oxidiser around when air was there for the taking, and his shell consisted of a central duct, a supply of fuel and an igniter. The inrush of air mixed with the fuel in a combustion chamber, was ignited, and the resultant efflux delivered thrust. Work began on developing shells in three calibres, 15cm, 21cm and 28cm, but the war ended before much had been done. No practical results of military worth were achieved, but theoretical deductions from the research carried out claimed a possible maximum range of 400km for a 28cm shell carrying a $28\frac{1}{2}$lb payload. Investigation into the principle continued in postwar years in both Britain and the United States, but the idea was eventually abandoned as not being worth the effort.

Gradually, as we have seen, research had moved away from the orthodox lines to become more and more concerned with ideas which, but for the stress of war, would never have been given a moment's thought by the military. But in wartime even the most outrageous idea, if well-presented in the right quarter, can be made to sound like the salvation of the nation, and the compartmentalised research field in Germany, together with the ambience of political infighting, was particularly receptive to the lunatic fringe of ordnance design. Probably the biggest white elephant was the multiple-chambered gun, though it was run very close by some equally wild ideas.

The multiple-chambered gun, it will be recalled, was proposed in Britain in 1940 (as it had been proposed on several earlier occasions) and was rejected by the Ordnance Board as being impractical (as it had been on several earlier occasions). But at about the same time that it appeared in Britain, a German engineer called Conders, chief engineer for the Rochling Stahlwerk, rediscovered the idea and began to work on it. In early 1943 he managed to persuade his company to make a 20mm calibre prototype which appeared to work sufficiently well to support his theories, and he then took his ideas to the top. By way of Speer, the idea was put to Hitler in the form of a fifty-barrel 15cm calibre unit buried in a hillside and aimed at London. This grandiose idea captured Hitler's imagination and he gave the necessary authority for work to begin, both on the gun and its ammunition and on the huge complex of concrete and steel required to emplace it. He also gave orders that the project was to be kept secret, so secret that the Army Weapons Office were not to know about it. The weapon was code-named the 'High Pressure Pump' and it later acquired the nicknames 'Busy Lizzie' and 'The Millipede' from its appearance, while to Hitler it became 'Vengeance Weapon 3' or 'V-3'.

A short 15cm trials gun was erected at the Artillery Proving Ground at Hillersleben, near Magdeburg, and this soon showed that there were a lot more problems in the design than had been anticipated. The propelling charges, arranged in side chambers and connecting with the bore, were originally intended to be fired sequentially by electricity, but Conders found, as the British Ordnance Board had foreseen, that accurate timing of ignition was impossible and the charges were simply ignited by the flash of the previous charge as the projectile passed each auxiliary chamber in turn. Then the shells were found to be unstable due to the design of folding fins being insufficiently rigid in flight, and the shell design had to begin again.

Now a full-sized 15cm gun was built at Misdroy, on the Baltic coast (where parts of it may still be found, rusting away in the undergrowth) and test firings began. The shells were still unstable in flight, and pressure waves in the barrel, caused by the interaction of the multiple

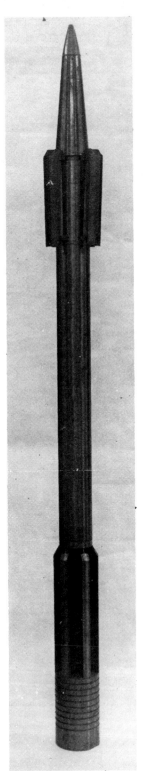

The experimental 15cm High Pressure Pump set up at Misdroy for firing tests. The auxiliary firing chambers extended both sides of the barrel, though in this picture some have been removed.

One design of shell for the 15cm High Pressure Pump. It weighed 183lb and was 92 inches long complete with the pusher piston at the base.

charges, burst the barrel every three or four shots. By this time too, the RAF had found the activity near Calais, where the 50-barrel installation was being prepared and, assuming it to be part of the V-1 pilotless bomb programme, bombed it into ruins.

The only thing which kept the project alive was Hitler's interest in it; nobody wanted to be the man who had to tell him the idea was a flop. Eventually the Army Weapons Office were brought in and experts re-designed the shell and gun and brought it to some semblance of reliability. But the final blow came when the Allied invasion overran the Calais area and the whole purpose behind the weapon disappeared. Two shortened versions were built and put into action during the last few weeks of the war, but there seems to have been little enthusiasm on the part of the operators; they deployed the guns as ordered, fired a handful of shells, then blew up the guns and retired. No records of performance or accuracy or effect were ever kept.

Running the 'High Pressure Pump' a close second in the credibility stakes was the Electric Gun. Ever since the solenoid was invented there have been proposals to use a magnetic field to launch a projectile, but the problem of generating the immense current needed was always a stumbling block. In 1943 an Engineer Muck, consultant to the Siemans Company, considered that advances in electrical technology now made the idea a practical one, and he submitted a grandiose scheme which, like the High Pressure Pump, envisaged a massive battery of solenoid guns emplaced in a hillside in France and aimed at London. This, he claimed, would launch a 450lb 15cm shell at 5,400ft/sec to a range of 155 miles; he forecast a rate of fire of half a million rounds a month, demanding a supply of 54,000 tons of coal to generate the necessary electric power.

Muck's paper was forwarded by the Munitions Ministry to some eminent scientists who soon demolished his theories, showing that some of his basic assumptions were erroneous. This, plus the fact that the V-2 rocket was almost ready for service, put an end to the idea. But at the same time another agency had, quite independently, also arrived at the electric gun idea. This was the 'Gesellschaft fur Geratbau', whose Engineer Hansler now proposed a weapon based on the principle of the linear motor, using a winged projectile resting on two bus-bars. This, he declared, would produce a 40mm weapon with a velocity of 6,500ft/sec, suitable as an anti-aircraft gun and demanding 3,900 kilowatts of power per gun. The arguments he put forward were so persuasive that the Luftwaffe gave a contract for the development of the gun. By March 1945 an experimental model had fired 5mm projectiles at 3,500ft/sec, and these results were considered sufficiently good to warrant issuing a specification for a 40mm gun firing a 14lb shell at 6,500ft/sec using a 10-metre 'barrel'. But like so many other ideas, the war ended before much more could be done, and the Hansler Electric Gun ended with it.

The only existing photograph of Doktor Zippermeyer's Vortex Cannon. Hot gas was expelled through the nozzle to create a whirlpool of air in the sky.

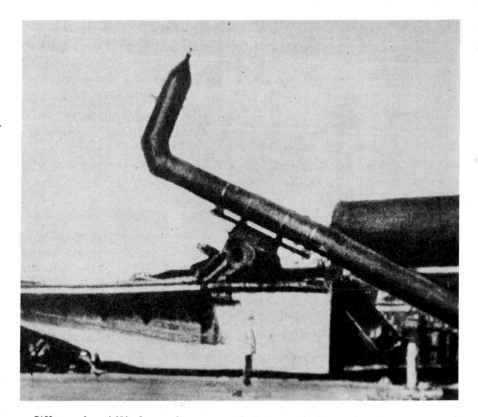

When the Allied armies entered Germany investigating teams of engineers and scientists followed closely behind in order to examine research and test establishments as they were over-run, and in this process some startling devices came to light. At the Artillery Proving Ground at Hillersleben, for example, they found 'an equipment which cannot be identified. It consists of an 8-foot cylinder with nozzles. . . made of boiler plate. Beside it was an L-shaped cylinder approximately 50 feet in length. . .' This turned out to be the 'Vortex Cannon', produced by the Forschungsinstitut Zippermeyer: the theory was that an explosive mixture would be fired in the small cylinder and the resulting rush of gas directed through the larger one so as to create a whirlpool of air in the sky which would cause an aircraft structure to be racked and strained to breaking point. Like most ordnance ideas, it was not new; in 1913 a Capt F. W. Barron of the Royal Garrison Artillery, in an essay on defence against aircraft, published in the 'Journal of the Royal Artillery' (Vol XL No. 6) wrote:

'Various expedients. . . add to the means of attacking hostile air vessels, such as torpedos, aerial mines, or an apparatus for creating vortex rings in the air with a view to upsetting the stability of warplanes. . .'

(It is worthy of note that an even earlier writer in the same Journal (Vol XL No. 3), a Major H. T. Hawkins RA (Retired) suggested 'we

might well have mobile aerial torpedos worked by wireless currents. . .'
Good gunners generally know what they need; the trouble lies in getting
the scientists to make the ideas work.)

Whether Dr Zippermeyer had read the RA Journal for 1913 is very
doubtful; in any event, though his vortex cannon worked, it did not
work sufficiently well to put the vortex up to the height at which aircraft
operated. The same institute was responsible for the 'Sound Cannon' in
which explosions fired in a reverberating chamber had their sound
magnified and directed by a parabolic mirror in an attempt to produce a
frequency capable of inducing injury to aircraft crews. Once again the
theory was impeccable and the device worked as planned in a laboratory
environment, but as a practical weapon it was a failure.

After this long catalogue of ever-wilder ideas which failed it will be
salutary to retire to a less rarified atmosphere and look at one or two
projects which worked, which were soundly based on reliable research,
which did exactly what their supporters claimed, and which became
viable weapons of war. One such text-book project was Britain's
improvements to the 3.7-inch anti-aircraft gun. As we have seen, this
stemmed from a 1928 specification which was worked on during the
early 1930s. In 1934 designs were prepared by Woolwich Arsenal and by
Vickers-Armstrong, and the Vickers design was accepted for production.
The first pilot model passed proof in April 1936 and production began
in April 1937, official service introduction being promulgated on 23
April 1937, and the first gun was issued in January 1938. This Mark 1
gun fired a 28lb shell at 2,600ft/sec to a maximum ceiling of 41,000 feet.

We should, perhaps, digress here to make clear what is meant by
'ceiling', since there are different definitions. The 'Maximum Ceiling' is
the greatest height to which the gun, at its maximum elevation, can
propel a shell; the only factors taken into account are the shell, the
cartridge and gravity. However, in the 1930s the actual height to which a
shell could go before detonating was governed by the maximum
operating time of the time fuze with which it was invariably fitted, and
the height at which the fuze ran out of time and burst the shell was
obviously the greatest height to which a combat-effective shell could be
fired. This became known as the 'Practical Ceiling' and in the case of the
3.7-inch it was 32,000 feet.

A little thought will show that the practical ceiling is only practical
for one shot; once the gun barrel moves away from the vertical, or from
its maximum elevation, as it would have to do in order to track a moving
aircraft, geometry shows that the practical ceiling must be lower. And
therefore there is a third ceiling known as the 'Effective Ceiling', the
definition of which depends upon who is doing the defining and when;'
what their tactical aspirations are and what sort of target they envisage.
The Japanese Naval Gunnery School at Tateyama gave the following
definition in 1944: 'The maximum altitude at which a directly

British 3.7-inch AA gun. In this picture it is being lined up by optical sight on coming into position. Firing data will be displayed to the gunlayer on the dials in front of him.

approaching aircraft flying at a ground speed of 300 mph can be engaged for 20 seconds, assuming the first round be fired at 30 second time of flight and the last at 70° elevation.' An American definition of about the same era was 'The height at which a 400 mph direct approacher can be engaged for 20 seconds up to a quadrant elevation of 70°' which adds up to much the same thing. Using this sort of definition, the effective ceiling of the 3.7-inch Mark I now becomes about 28,000 feet.

The Mark 1 gun was hand-loaded to give a rate of fire of about ten rounds a minute. This was later improved by the adoption of a mechanical fuze-setter/loader which doubled the rate of fire, and wartime fuze improvements slightly raised the effective ceiling. It was, without doubt, the best weapon of its type in the world at the start of the war, but it was obvious that the rate of improvement of aircraft would leave the gun behind within the next two or three years. Accordingly in January 1941 the War Office demanded a weapon with a ceiling of 50,000 feet, a velocity giving a time of flight of 30 seconds to that height, and the capability of firing three rounds in 20 seconds with a fourth round loaded. The choices available to meet this demand narrowed down to four. First, the existing Naval 5.25-inch High Angle gun; second, a 5.25-inch with a barrel liner of 4.5-inch calibre; third, a 5.25-inch with a 3.7-inch barrel; and fourth, a 4.5-inch gun linered down to 3.7-inch calibre. 'Linering down' meant reducing the barrel calibre without reducing the chamber dimensions, so that the smaller shell would be propelled by the larger cartridge. It might be said that there was good precedent for this; the most successful British AA gun of the First World War had been a 3.3-inch 18-pounder linered to 3-inch calibre to fire the 13-pounder shell.

The Naval 5.25-inch gun, which fired an 80lb shell at 2,800ft/sec to achieve an effective ceiling of 43,000 feet was by far the most attractive proposition, but it was going to take a long time to design and produce a suitable static mounting for land service use, and in the interim the 4.5 linered down to 3.7 was selected as a stop-gap weapon. In order to improve the ballistics, the 3.7-inch barrel was completely re-designed for this new application, being lengthened by 57 inches and rifled in accordance with a system developed by Col. G. O. C. Probert of the Armament Research Department. In this the rifling grooves gradually shallowed as they approached the muzzle, the last three calibres, length being smoothbored. The shell's driving band was thus squeezed down flush with the shell body so that it emerged from the muzzle with no excrescences to affect the airflow; moreover the effect of the reduction of groove diameter was, in a small way, similar to the effect of a taper-bore and made a contribution to improving the velocity.

The 3.7-inch Mark 6 gun, basically a 4.5-inch fitted with a 3.7-inch barrel. Being a statically-mounted weapon, weight was less of a problem than with mobile equipments, and instead of using springs or pneumatic balancing devices to counter the muzzle preponderance, a massive counter-weight is slung behind the breech.

This new barrel was allied to a chamber and breech based on the 4.5-inch AA gun, though in fact the cartridge case was longer and thinner than that of the 4.5-inch. The mounting adopted was the standard 4.5-inch static mounting, and the final product became the 3.7-inch Mark 6 gun, entering service in 1943. Firing the improved 28lb shell at 3,470ft/sec it had a maximum ceiling of 59,300 feet and an effective ceiling of 45,000feet, and a rate of fire of 19 rounds a minute. It was so good, in fact, that when the 5.25-inch gun finally came into service towards the end of the war, it never supplanted the 3.7-inch Mark 6, which lasted until the end of the anti-aircraft gun era; indeed, the 3.7 had the last word, being declared obsolete on 20th May 1959, eight days after the obsoletion of the 5.25-inch!

In the anti-aircraft battle the problem of providing suitable guns was the least of the worries; Britain, the U.S.A. and Germany all produced excellent weapons. The principal problem was putting the guns to effective use by bursting shells on the target, and here there were many variables and imponderables which altered the equation. The basic problem was to estimate the position of the aircraft as it would be by the time the shell had reached the same altitude and then point the gun so as to put the shell within lethal distance of the target and burst it there. Such questions as the fall-off in velocity as the gun wore out – a rapid process with high-velocity weapons having a high rate of fire in night-long engagements – the effect of atmospheric conditions on the shell's flight and the estimation of aircraft speed and direction could be, to some extent, allowed for. What was less controllable was the performance of the shell's time fuze. This was set, before loading, to the predicted time of flight to the target, with an added allowance for 'dead time', the time which would elapse between setting the fuze and actually firing the shell away. With hand loading this was an approximation, but the arrival of mechanical fuze-setter-loader devices gave a fixed and constant dead time which improved accuracy. Nevertheless, the clockwork mechanism of the fuze had a margin of error which meant that the point of burst could well be one or two hundred feet above or below the target even if every other source of error were eliminated. And since the lethal burst radius of the shell was only about 50 feet, such errors were by no means negligible.

During the war the German designers began work on sub-calibre anti-aircraft projectiles, as we have seen, and also on an 'intermediate calibre' gun, and in both these projects the standard shell filling was set at 500 grammes of high explosive, this being considered sufficient to deliver lethal damage to a four-engined bomber. But such a size brought the lethal radius down to a much smaller figure, which in turn decreased the chance of damaging a target. A Dr Voss, research scientist with the Reichs Luftministerium considered this and produced a closely-reasoned paper which argued that since the chance of placing such a

small shell close to the target was very little different from the chance of obtaining a direct hit, it followed that by doing away with time fuzes and fitting shells with simple impact fuzes the errors inherent in the fuze mechanism, in the computation of fuze length and in the setting machines would all be removed, the rate of fire would be vastly improved, and, mathematically at least, the chances of damaging a target would be considerably increased.

Such a startling theory as this was a bit much for the Luftwaffe gunners to accept at one gulp, but Voss's arguments were so well-constructed and persuasive that a scientific panel was set up to examine the theory and a number of firing trials were carried out. The results showed that Voss's theories had, if anything, been pessimistic, and the system promised a startling increase in the effectiveness of anti-aircraft fire. To begin with, Luftwaffe batteries were ordered to set their time fuzes at lesser ranges, and fire without using the machine fuze setters. It took some argument with die-hard gunners before this lesson was assimilated, but it was eventually tried and good results were obtained. A massive conversion programme of fuzes was begun, fitting sensitive impact units in the nose and rendering the clocks inoperative, an interim measure until new impact-only fuzes could be provided, and on 20 March 1945 the Luftwaffe issued orders to completely abandon the use of time fuzes in high explosive shell. Unfortunately the change was made too late to have much effect on affairs, and the chaotic conditions at the end of the war prevented any records of the system's effectiveness ever coming to light.

On the Allied side the same problem was approached from a totally different angle: if setting the fuze caused errors, then let the fuze set itself. During the early days of radar, in 1938, scientists exposed to the problems of gunnery for the first time soon fastened on to the fuze as a prime source of error, and it occurred to some of them that it might be possible to apply electronics to the task. The flying target was being 'illuminated' by radar and a small portion of the emitted signal was being reflected by the target; might it not be possible to design a fuze which would react to this reflected signal and detonate the shell within lethal distance of the target?

Unfortunately the strength of the reflection was measured in microwatts or less, and the circuitry necessary to detect and amplify such minute signals was impossible to compress into the amount of space available in a shell fuze. The next idea was to produce a simple transmitter and receiver which would go inside a fuze so that it sent its own signals out and, when a reflection was detected, burst the shell. This seemed more feasible, provided certain components, as yet never built or even invented, could be produced, such as tiny electronic valves, miniature batteries and so forth. And of course, always supposing the whole assembly could stand being fired out of a gun.

By this time it was 1940 and the British electronics industry was at full stretch providing military radio and radar, while the research and development facilities were also hard pressed. There was no research capacity available to take the 'proximity fuze' idea any further; and even had there been, there were certainly no facilities for manufacturing them in the hundreds of thousands needed for such an application. At this point the Tizard Commission went to the United States to try and enlist scientific support; this visit is probably best remembered for the revelation of the cavity magnetron, which advanced American radar research overnight. One of the less-publicised items passed over by the Tizard party was the specifications and calculations which had been done on the proximity fuze. In the parcelling-out of projects afterwards, the U.S. Navy took over responsibility for the fuze and placed development contracts with Eastman Kodak for the overall design, Sylvania for the valves and electronic components, and Exide for the batteries. An immense amount of effort went into the project and by June 1943 the proximity fuze was an accomplished fact and was in service with the U.S. Navy in the Pacific.

With Naval supplies assured, designs were then drawn up for fuzes suited to the various U.S. and British Army anti-aircraft guns; although the fuze was now a working device, each different calibre of gun had to have its own model, designed to suit the velocity, spin rate and shell size, and each model had to be separately developed and perfected. As luck would have it the 3.7-inch AA gun fuzes were completed and put into production just in time to be used against the V-1 Flying Bomb in 1944, though as someone once said in another military context, it was a damned close-run thing.

With the proximity (or 'Peter' or 'Pozit' or 'VT' — it had a variety of cover-names at various times) fuze an article of standard issue, the U.S. Army now contemplated a new approach to anti-aircraft gun design. Until now the limiting factor on the gun's rate of fire had been the time needed to set the fuze; without the need for fuze setting it should be possible to increase the rate of fire by a significant amount. Accordingly, in August 1944, an 'urgent request' was made for a 'Short and Intermediate Range AA Gun compatible with VT fuzes and having on-carriage fire control.' Pilot models, both towed and self-propelled, were authorised at high priority. In fact, although the minutes of the U.S. Ordnance Committee contained the above phrases in August, it seems highly likely that the request had been made, perhaps unofficially, some time before, since in September it was reported that the design was nearing completion at Watervliet Arsenal, and a weapon as complex as this one promised to be was hardly to be run up in a month or six weeks' time.

Be that as it may, a design of 75mm gun with mechanical loading from two revolver-type magazines on a towed mounting complete with radar, optical tracker and predictor/computor was soon on paper. By January 1945 the gun and loading gear were built and undergoing test. This was the 75mm Gun T22, the mount being designated T19, but gun proof showed that the muzzle velocity was only 2,300ft/sec, a poor performance for a modern weapon, and by June the programme (now less vital due to the end of the war in Europe) was put back to allow a re-design of the gun to try and reach 3,000ft/sec. A T22E2 gun, ten calibres longer, was authorised in September 1945 and development then continued into the postwar years, the weapon finally reaching service as the M51 'Skysweeper' in the early 1950s. In production form it fired at 45 rounds a minute, amply demonstrating the validity of the reasoning which began it, though it only ever achieved 2,800ft/sec, with a maximum ceiling of 30,000 feet.

It will have been noted that the initial demand for the T22 75mm gun called for pilot models both towed and self-propelled. To the best of my knowledge no self-propelled version ever appeared, even in pilot form, which is surprising; with the American expertise in, and love of, the automotive field, practically every other piece of ordnance, with the exception of heavy coast guns, found itself on a self-propelled mounting sooner or later.

With a few minor exceptions, all self-propelled guns were wartime creations, and they coalesced into well-defined groups which reflect national thinking on the subject. There are, naturally, exceptions which prove the rule, but in general the German and Russian approach differed in its tactical concept from American and British ideas. In Germany the self-propelled gun was, primarily, an assault gun; direct-firing at short range, its task was to accompany the infantry advance rather than the armour, in order to provide instantly available heavy firepower to deal with strongpoints impeding the progress of the infantry advance. The Russians adopted a similar view-point, partly because the Germans seemed to get results and also because the philosophy of direct contact and support suited their simple and direct tactics in the attack. The other German application of the self-propelled gun was in the 'tank destroyer' role, but here the line between artillery and tank becomes very indistinct and most of this class of vehicles, as for example the 88mm-armed 'Ferdinand', are more usually considered to be specialist, limited-traverse tanks.

The most remarkable German SP development was the enormous 'Karl' howitzer, one of the exceptions which was designed as an indirect-fire weapon. It was first demanded by the German Army in 1935 as a heavy 60cm (23.6-inch) calibre siege howitzer to deal with fortifications which could not conveniently be dealt with by railway artillery. This request in itself is not without interest; an examination of a railway map of Europe leads to the conclusion that even in 1935 eyes were looking east, where railway lines were fewer and farther between than they were

The German 'Karl'
60cm howitzer firing
on Sebastopol. The
ammunition carrier
stands to one side
with its supply crane
ready to swing
another two-ton
shell across.

on the borders of France or Belgium.

The first weapon was completed by Rheinmettal-Borsig in 1939, and after a series of trials two service weapons were completed, known as the 'Karl II' series. These, christened 'Thor' and 'Eva', were completed early in 1941 and were later employed against Sebastopol and Leningrad. They were effective, if cumbersome, weapons: firing a 1.55-ton high explosive shell at 925ft/sec they had a range of 7,325 yards, while with a 2.16-ton concrete-piercing shell the range was a mere 4,920 yards. Consquently the Army opined that a reduction in shell weight would be acceptable if it were accompanied by an increase in range. Rheinmettal therefore set about building four more chassis and developed a 54cm (21.25-inch) calibre barrel, the external dimensions of which were the same as those of the 60cm model so that the two could be interchanged on any mounting. The exact number of barrels of each calibre which were made remains in some doubt, since they were interchanged from time to time. The 54cm barrel was provided with a 1.3-ton concrete-piercing shell which ranged to 11,485 yards.

The chassis for these weapons was a simple steel box divided into three compartments. The forward compartment carried the Mercedes-Benz V-12 diesel engine and transmission; the centre compartment supported the gun and also carried a carriage recoil system; while the third compartment carried the vehicle batteries and a reduction gear for raising and lowering the hull. When going into action a power take-off from the engine was engaged with this gearing and, through connect-

ing linkages, rotated the vehicle bogie wheel torsion bar anchorages. This allowed the bogie wheels to move up and the hull to sink until it rested on the ground and relieved the suspension of the 123-ton weight and the firing shock. The firing shock was also reduced by a dual recoil system; a normal hydro-pneumatic system was interposed between the gun and its mounting, and another system operated between the mounting and the chassis.

For movement there were three options: for short distances it could of course drive on its own tracks; for longer moves by road the weapon was dismantled, the top carriage, gun and carriage recoil system became three separate loads each carried on a 16-wheel transporter while the chassis was winched on to a 24-wheel trailer and towed by a Hanomag tractor. For long moves by rail the complete equipment was fitted with a cantilever arm attached to each end of the hull. Using hydraulic jacks the entire unit was then lifted until two special railway wagons could be run under the cantilever arms, after which the assembly was lowered until the arms located on pivots on the wagons and the gun vehicle was suspended between them.

The 'Karl' equipments were masterly technical achievements but, having said that, there is little else to praise; the amount of action they saw and the effect they had was in no proportion to the effort which went into their design and manufacture.

British self-propelled gun design was hampered by the need to produce tanks first and foremost, and since tank production was a long time in reaching anything like the demand which existed, and since the tank designers were making heavy weather of producing a reliable tank, it is not surprising that little ever appeared in the way of an all-British self-propelled gun. True, there were a surprising variety of pilot models and small runs, conversions of existing armoured vehicles of which there happened to be sufficiency, but these were mainly retained for Home Defence. The first SP proposals were applications of the 'tank destroyer' theory, light, fast vehicles carrying anti-tank guns, which could rove around looking for tanks; at the time, this was envisaged as likely to happen in Suffolk and Kent against the expected Panzer divisions and there was little available equipment. These first SPs were, therefore, two-pounder guns grafted to Lloyd carriers in a variety of ways. When the six-pounder gun began to appear, the tank destroyer theory was still active, and the gun was mounted into all sorts of chassis; the 10-ton AEC 'Matador' truck, the Humber armoured car, a special armoured and wheeled chassis from Morris which was called the 'Firefly', and finally an armoured shield mounting on the rear end of a Chevrolet 30cwt truck chassis. This latter model appeared to be the best of the bunch, and under the name of 'Deacon' entered service in some numbers in 1941. Several were sent to North Africa and the Western Desert where they gave reasonably good service.

A two-pounder mounted on a Lloyd carrier, one of the early wartime attempts at self-propelled anti-tank artillery. There were numerous variations on this design but few saw service.

Another attempt to bestow mobility on an anti-tank gun was 'Deacon', a six-pounder on a Chevrolet chassis. These were used with some success in the latter parts of the Desert campaign in 1942-3.

Another method of moving the 17-pounder was the 'Straussler' mounting, whch added wheels and an engine to a highly modified gun carriage.

A top view of the Straussler mounting, showing its arrangement. The prospect of trying to conceal this machine, particularly by digging it into a pit, was the principal objection to it.

    With the arrival of the 17-pounder anti-tank gun late in 1942 came the decision to design a 'proper' SP chassis, since the size and power of the 17-pounder was against such extempore lash-ups as sufficed for smaller guns, and a tracked vehicle with 360° traverse for the gun was demanded. This was sailing close to the wind, since it was obviously going to finish up looking very much like a tank and a fair amount of diplomacy would be needed to make sure the Royal Artillery kept it, since the Royal Armoured Corps would, if it turned out to be any good, make a strong claim for it. Eventually the A30 chassis was selected in 1943, with the hope of reaching production in 1944, but the RA were no more lucky in production of tracked vehicles than were the RAC, and the 'Avenger' SP

gun never reached the troops until the war was well over.

As an interim measure – a well-worn phrase in British equipment development – numbers of obsolescent 'Valentine' tank chassis were taken and reworked to take the 17-pounder gun in a limited-traverse mounting firing towards the rear. If nothing else, this configuration prevented any attempt at driving into battle with the gun blazing and usurping the function of the tanks; which is probably why the RAC raised no objections. Awkward as it sounds, the 'Archer' SP was a highly effective weapon and saw much use in North-West Europe.

In the field artillery sphere the long-suffering Lloyd carrier had a 25-pounder gun fitted into it, alongside the driver, but this appears to have been no more than a one-off experiment. In October 1941 a decision was taken to manufacture 100 25-pounder SPs, basing the vehicle on the 'Valentine' tank chassis. The turret was removed and a large, square, armoured box placed on top; into this went the 25-pounder. With 8° of traverse and only 15° of elevation, due to the armoured box, the maximum range was only 6,400 yards, severely limiting the usefulness of the equipment. It was used in North Africa by the British 1st Army, and it provided some useful lessons in the handling and organization of self-propelled field artillery, but that is about as much as can charitably be said about it. 'Bishop', as it was named, did not even survive the war, being made obsolete in October 1944, one of the very few weapons to be scrapped while the war was still in progress.

'Bishop' was the last British design of field artillery SP equipment to

'Bishop', the self-propelled 25-pounder mounted on a Valentine tank chassis. The gun's elevation was restricted, which prevented the full ballistic potential being realised.

'Alecto', a proposed airborne support weapon using a 95mm howitzer in the chassis of the 'Tetrarch' tank.

'Sexton', the 25-pounder on the chassis of the redundant 'Ram' tank. A very good weapon, it remained in British service until the middle 1950s and is still, in 1976, in service with the Portuguese Army.

One of the less-likely applications of self-propulsion was this combination of a 25-pounder on top of a DUKW. The intention was to provide last-minute support in an amphibious attack, but it was never adopted.

The quick way to mobility, demonstrated by the U.S. Army in 1941. The 105mm Howitzer Motor Carriage T19 consisted of the standard 105mm howitzer grafted on to the standard half-track reconnaisance car. The 75mm gun and the six-pounder anti-tank gun were similarly mounted.

enter service for nearly thirty years; the weapon which replaced it, 'Sexton', was based on a Canadian adaptation of an American chassis. The Canadian government had rushed headlong into tank production with a design called the 'Ram', based on the American 'Sherman' chassis

American 3-inch M10 tank destroyers employed as field artillery in Italy in September 1944.

'Priest', the American HMC M7 105mm howitzer. The machine gun barbette which gave it the nickname can be seen on the left of the howitzer.

Self-propulsion was also applied to anti-aircraft guns with the object of protecting columns on the move. This is the American twin-40mm SP M19 or 'Duster'. As well as its anti-aircraft role it was an extremely potent assault gun.

but with a Canadian design of turret mounting a six-pounder gun. By the time the design was cleared and production facilities prepared, it was apparent that 'Ram' was under-gunned, so the basic chassis was re-worked to remove the turret and build up the superstructure to accept the 25-pounder gun in an open-topped armoured barbette. With the full elevation of the gun now available, together with 50° of traverse, the maximum performance could be used and 'Sexton' entered service in September 1943. It was an excellent weapon, and it served until the middle 1950s when its place was taken by the American 155mm Howitzer M44.

American SP design began on more or less the same lines as British with a variety of extemporized models, most of which appeared to have the Tank Destroyer image well to the fore. The earliest to appear in service was the 75mm gun mounted on a half-track as the 'Gun Motor Carriage M3'. The first of these were sent to the Philippines in the autumn of 1941 and proved useful as tank destroyers during the Japanese invasion of the following year. Less successful was the 3-inch AA gun mounted as an anti-tank weapon on top of a 'Cletrac' commercial tracked tractor; it was hurriedly standardized in 1942, but on second thoughts it was realized that such an unprotected weapon was unsuitable and only the pilot model was ever made. Another

entertaining idea was the Gun Motor Carriage T8, a 37mm anti-tank gun mounted on a Ford 'Swamp Buggy'. More serious was the Howitzer Motor Carriage T19, the standard U.S. 105mm howitzer mounted, like the 75mm gun, on a half-track scout car chassis. This was never standardized but a small number were built and in 1942 these went with the invasion troops to North Africa where, like the British 'Bishop' in the same theatre, they were useful in teaching lessons about the handling of SP equipments.

It would serve no useful purpose, apart from record and entertainment, to catalogue the enormous number of SP developments which were born in the U.S.A. between 1942 and 1945; it runs well into three figures, but we must content ourselves with noticing the ones which went to war and gave some account of themselves. In the anti-tank role the most successful was the Gun Motor Carriage M10, based on the M4A2 tank chassis and armed with the 3-inch gun M7. Standardized in November 1943, it was issued both to U.S. and British units, but the British soon removed the 3-inch and replaced it with the 17-pounder, a much more potent weapon. The Americans admitted the logic of this and re-designed the equipment to use their 90mm gun, calling the result GMC M36.

The standard 105mm howitzer was mounted into the M3 tank chassis to become the HMC M7, and the first production of these was shipped to the Eighth Army in Egypt in time to take part in the Alamein battle and the subsequent advance across Cyrenaica. This was a first-class weapon; it was provided with a peculiar pulpit-like anti-aircraft machine gun barbette alongside the howitzer, which gave rise to its nickname of 'Priest' in British service; this appears to have been the innocent beginning of the practice of bestowing clerical names on British SP guns.

The Americans were not content with putting their field howitzer on tracks; they felt that medium guns could usefully be mobilized to accompany armoured formations, and the quickest solution was to take some of the many obsolescent 155mm GPF guns and mount them on a suitable chassis. The GPF – more correctly the M1918 – was a French equipment adopted during the First World War, and it was being rapidly replaced in the towed role by the 155mm Gun M1. In 1942 the M1918 gun was mounted, very simply, in a chassis derived from the M3 tank, to become the GMC M12, and its basic design was so sound that the layout adopted has been retained ever since. The gun was mounted on a pedestal in a flat working area at the rear of the chassis; there was no armour protection, and the firing shock was resisted by a firing spade at the rear which resembled a bulldozer blade. On arriving at the firing position this blade was lowered and the vehicle reversed so as to dig the blade into the ground; thereafter the firing shock passed into the ground and the suspension was relieved of excess strain.

The M1918 gun, though, was outclassed by this time, its ammunition

was gradually running out, and the design of the mounting prevented the full range being reached; so, as it seemed to be a successful weapon in other respects, a new design was begun in March 1944, using the M1 gun. The first attempt was the T89, using a special chassis made up from components designed for the T23 light tank; this was an elegant specification using electric drive transmission, but it was too good to be true and failed to pass the approving authority. The T89 was abandoned, and in March 1944 work began on the T83; this was more conventional, using the M4 tank chassis. The gun was pedestal mounted, as had been the M12, but in such a manner as to allow 60° of elevation and the full range of the gun. Procurement of five pilot equipments was authorised in June 1944; in the following month approval was given for 304 more, and in April 1945 the order was increased to 600 weapons and the T83 was standardised as the M40.

The American 155mm SP M40, a combination of the standard 155mm Gun M1, a pedestal mounting originally conceived as a coast-defence measure, and the chassis of the M4 medium tank.

With a weapon capable of 25,000 yards range now on tracks, it would have been reasonable if the Americans had stopped there; but they now

The U.S. 240mm Howitzer SP T92, built by placing the howitzer barrel and recoil system on to a chassis derived from the M26 heavy tank. It weighed 56 tons; the war ended before it could be standardised and brought into use.

Rear view of the 8-inch SP howitzer M43 showing the recoil spade and the ample working space obtained by relocating the engine in a midships position.

The German LG40
75mm recoilless gun
as used in Crete. The
blast through the
venturi at the left
counterbalanced the
discharge of the
shell.

An experimental
German recoilless
gun, demonstrating
its lightness due to
the absence of a
recoil system.

had the bit between their teeth. The 8-inch howitzer was interchangeable with the 155mm gun of the towed mounting; it was logical, therefore, to do the same with the SP mounting, and the HMC T89 was developed more or less in step with the 155mm T83. Shortly after standardisation of the M40, 576 8-inch T89s were authorised, and in September 1945 it was standardised as the M43.

The largest equipments in American field service were the partner 8 inch gun and 240mm howitzer, and in January 1944 the development of SP mountings for these two weapons was authorised. Using a specially-strengthened chassis based on various production components for the M26 tank, the two weapons were successfully mounted, the 8-inch gun becoming the GMC T93 and the 240mm howitzer the HMC T92. By March 1945 the designs were cleared and limited procurement of 115 T92 and 58 T93 authorised; in the following month these figures were increased to 144 and 72 respectively. The first pilot models were delivered in June and production was scheduled to continue into 1946. But the end of the war arrived before more than half-a-dozen of each had been made and the production schedule was cancelled, the intention now being to submit the completed weapons to more searching and leisurely trials before deciding on their future. Although the trials were successful, the postwar army felt that there was little use for the weapons and no more were ever made.

Finally in this parade of inventiveness, we should look at a collection of ideas concerned with making guns more efficient in other directions than simply performance. One of the principal reasons for guns weighing as much as they do is the need to make provision for the sudden shock of discharge when the gun is fired, the shock generally called 'recoil'. Some idea of the nature of this shock can be grasped by analogy: the force to be absorbed when an 8-inch howitzer recoils is of the same order as the stopping of a fifty-ton locomotive from a speed of fifty miles an hour in a space of four feet. The mechanism needed to deal with this force must therefore be extremely strong and it follows from that that it must also be heavy. By doing away with this mechanism a considerable weight can be saved.

The general principals and development of the recoilless gun are fairly well known, beginning with the American Cleland-Davis countershot gun of 1913 and coming to practical life with the German 'Light Guns' used in Crete, the British 'Burney' guns, and the American 'Kromuskit' guns during the 1939-45 period. These wartime weapons all relied, by one system or another, on discharging a stream of gas to the rear, venting it through venturi jets so as to develop a forward thrust equivalent to the rearward thrust arising from the discharge of the projectile. But there were other attempts at making recoilless guns working on different principles which are worth recording. One such was a proposal by a M. de Normanville in October 1940, of which a report said

The built-in defect of the recoilless gun — its back-blast — is well shown by this photograph of the turf torn up behind a British 7.2-inch model.

'This is a proposal to use a gun of which the barrel is not restrained. The barrel will therefore be ejected towards the rear with the same momentum as that imparted to the projectile, so that the gun is capable of firing only one round. Its use mounted in the wings of aircraft, as suggested by the inventor, is obviously out of the question . . .' It obviously was, but with a little amendment it could have been made to work as, indeed, the German Rheinmettal company had already proved – though this was, of course, unknown in England at the time. Rheinmettal, approached by the Luftwaffe with a request for an airborne gun capable of damaging a battleship, had developed a massive 35cm (13.77-inch) recoilless gun carried by a Dornier Do.217 bomber. The gun fired a 1,400lb piercing shell and the recoil was balanced off by the rearward ejection of a 1,400lb cartridge case. Although the weapon was perfected before the outbreak of war, the Luftwaffe lost interest and the weapon was never used, but smaller guns on a similar principle, ejecting a specially massive cartridge case to counterbalance the shot ejection, were developed later in the war for the armament of fighter aircraft and a few were used in combat.

One of the rare instances of Italian unorthodox development was also in the recoilless gun field. This was the 'Pezzani' gun, discovered in Italy in 1944. It used two cartridges, one in a conventional chamber to propel the shell and one in an auxiliary chamber open at the rear to provide the counter-thrust. Both charges were fired simultaneously by electricity. It was claimed that this system of operation allowed the full development of the gun's ballistic potential, whereas a normal recoilless gun, since it used a portion of the propelling charge to produce the rearward blast, invariably reduced the possible performance; there seems to be an element of special pleading in this argument. The Pezzani gun was proposed principally for aircraft use, though it could equally well have been applied to a field weapon. Pezzani interested the Luftwaffe in his design and it is believed the Rheinmettal company took the idea up, but no practical weapon ever resulted.

One of the probable reasons why the German scientists never followed up the Pezzani idea was the acute shortage of propellant powder by the end of 1944. Running a war on three fronts demanded colossal quantities of explosives, and while it was possible to economise in high explosives by developing various admixtures of slightly lesser efficiency, no such adulteration was possible in propellants. The recoilless gun had an unsupportable appetite for propellant; the standard field howitzer, the 105mm Model 18, used a 2.77lb cartridge to propel a 32lb shell to 11,675 yards, while the recoilless equivalent, the 105mm LG40, required 6.82lb to send the same shell to 8,695 yards. The disproportion in 75mm calibre was even worse; 2.51 ounces for the 75mm Infantry Gun 18, 2.71lb for the 75mm LG40 recoilless gun. Since recoilless guns were of little tactical importance in 1944 – they had been developed for airborne use

and by that time there was no German airborne force left worth speaking of – this demand for propellant led to the cessation of ammunition manufacture in the autumn of 1944 and the recoilless guns went into retirement as the ammunition stocks ran out.

The German 8cm PAW 'High and Low Pressure' gun, exhibited at Aberdeen Proving Ground, USA.

It was doubly unfortunate that this should happen just when the German infantry were loudly demanding a lightweight anti-tank gun. They had been offered the existing recoilless guns but had turned them down since, being short barrelled weapons, their short-range accuracy was simply not good enough. Nor were rockets regarded with much favour; shoulder-fired rocket launchers were available but these were for extremely short range firing only, and something capable of reaching to 500 metres or so was needed; at this sort of range the accuracy of a rocket was poor. The problem was passed to various ordnance companies, the only stipulations being that the weapon had to be light and handy, it had to use less propellant than a rocket or recoilless gun, and it had to be capable of hitting a one-metre-square target at 750 metres range without fail.

The Rheinmettal-Borsig company had, for some time, been experimenting with a new idea in ballistics and they now applied it to this demand to produce a totally new type of weapon. The principle is known as the 'High and Low Pressure System' and the weapon was called the 8cm PAW (Panzer Abwehr Werfer) 600. The gun was a smoothbore with an exceptionally thin and light barrel and a strengthened breech and chamber section. The round of ammunition consisted of a cartridge case with a heavy steel plate at the mouth, pierced with a number of venturis. Attached to this plate by a shearable pin was a fin-stabilised hollow charge bomb. When the round was loaded the bomb entered the smoothbore barrel while the cartridge closing plate abutted against a shoulder at the front of the chamber. On firing, the propellant exploded inside the case and generated a gas pressure of about 8 tons to the square inch. The gas then passed through the restricting jets in the closing plate to develop a lower pressure, about three tons, behind the projectile. As this pressure built up, so the pin sheared and the projectile was propelled up the bore, generating space behind it faster than the gas could flow through the restricting jets, so that by the time it left the muzzle the pressure was down to about one ton.

This weapon fulfilled all the requirements: it weighed only 1,322lb, the charge was only 11 ounces, and it was accurate. The 8cm model went into service in December 1944, 260 guns being built before production stopped in March 1945. A 105mm version was under development, but this only reached the prototype stage before the war ended.

Strangely, little use has been made of this system since the war; the U.S. Army made a 40mm shoulder-fired grenade launcher using the idea, and the Swiss Army fitted a High and Low Pressure Gun in an armoured vehicle for a short period; as this is being written it is learned that a new Soviet airborne tracked carrier is armed with a 73mm gun using the system.

This, however, is typical of much of the wartime development. When the war ended research projects were ruthlessly cut, and any idea which seemed to hold little promise was axed on the spot. Those applications which had shown some combat effectiveness or which had been brought almost to production were allowed to continue, though in many cases the planned production was halted so that the whole design could be re-appraised in a more leisurely and scientific manner and, if necessary, modifications made to the design. To quote but one example: when the war ended Britain was on the point of producing a number of recoilless guns together with their special plastic-explosive-filled 'Wall-buster' shells. This programme was stopped, only sufficient weapons and ammunition for trial purposes being made. The whole system was then placed under investigation and it was another ten years before recoilless guns entered service – admittedly, of far better design, reflecting the research which had gone on in the interval. Today very little artillery equipment can be said to have descended directly from wartime developments; recoilless guns, discarding sabot shot, squashhead shells, and proximity fuzes are about all. But on the other hand there are few guns or projectiles which do not incorporate in their design, be it ever so technical a point or well hidden a feature, which does not owe something to the scientists and engineers of the war years.

Chapter 4
THE PROOF OF THE PUDDING

It has been said, and it sounds reasonable, that there was never a day from the commencement of the Second World War until its end which did not see artillery being fired in combat somewhere in the world, and it would be invidious to attempt to write chronologically of the war's progress in terms of artillery engagements. Furthermore field artillery actions, except in such dire and unusual situations as that of 155 Battery at Sidi Nisr, rarely lend themselves to stirring narrative. The story of field artillery handling and tactics throughout the course of the war is essentially one of improvements in target location, communication and control until, by the end, the power of artillery was sufficient to decide the course of a battle almost irrespective of what the remainder of the armies did. This may appear to be a sweeping and partisan statement,

A British 4.5 firing at dusk in the advance to the Mareth Line.

but it is borne out by investigations made during and after battles and which were carried out by the Army Operational Research Group (AORG) of the British Army. In one of their final memoranda they observed that, in respect of various actions analysed, 'any difference in enemy resistance or our own troops' progress would be largely the result of differences in the type or amount of artillery support.'

The AORG applied statistical and scientific method to analysing the results of field artillery fire, and some of the results, while tending to bear out opinions which professional artillerymen instinctively held, were nevertheless surprising. The usual criteria for the power of an artillery bombardment had always been the number of guns, or the weight of ammunition fired, or the ratio of guns to front. Now a new and more accurate figure appeared for the first time, the actual weight of shells per square kilometer of target. In north-west Europe this figure was deduced for a number of actions, and the number of casualties incurred by British troops in the attack – a measure of the defensive effort of the German defenders – was also calculated. A specimen table reads as follows:

Weight of bombardment tons/sq km	Average casualties per infantry battalion in the attack
50–100	26
100–150	18
150–200	15
200+	13

As the reports pointed out, there is a law of diminishing returns at work here. An attack without any artillery support at all would undoubtedly produce a high casualty rate; up to 100 tons/km^2 brings the rate down to 26. After that the improvement becomes less and less as the weight of shells increases. Generally, it seemed that a level of about 50 tons/km^2 was sufficient; more shelling rarely produced a spectacular collapse of the defenders, while it generally meant that the greater quantity of ammunition was dispersed more widely about its targets in accordance with the well-known laws of probability and distribution, which in turn led to the attacking infantry leaving a greater gap between themselves and the bombardment. This led to greater delay in getting to grips with the enemy after the bombardment stopped, in which time the defenders had time to collect their wits and their weapons and set about making their defence felt. Further analyses of this point indicated that if the attack was as much as 30 minutes behind the bombardment, the effect of the artillery fire was reduced by a factor of four or five, and that even five or ten minutes' delay detracted from the effect of the artillery preparation.

This aspect was, of course, appreciated long ago; but with the intense weight of shelling being produced by massed artillery towards the end of the war it was brought into new focus. Another age-old controversy which was revived was the argument as to the relative worth of one large shell as opposed to a number of smaller ones. The value of heavy shell was indisputable when it came to doing material damage, as this report on the Mareth Line battle in North Africa pointed out:

'When . . . the regiment passed through the Mareth Line we quickly realized that the great number of 25-pounder shells fired into it had done nothing beyond local neutralization, with perhaps a little damage to the field defences between the forts. Where cupolas and concrete dug-outs had been cracked open, it was by 5.5-inch shells. . .'

But when it came to anti-personnel effect, it seemed that what counted most was not the pure tonnage of explosive but the number of individual shells which burst on the target; a ton of ammunition delivered as 90 25-pounder shells gave far more result than a ton in the form of 22 5.5-inch shells. Appreciation of this led to the invention of the 'Pepperpot' concentration of fire, in which every available weapon, irrespective of its arms of service or normal role, joined in the firing. In Operation 'Veritable' the 51st (Highland), 53rd (Welsh), 15th (Scottish) and 2nd (Canadian) Divisions attacked between Wyler and Grafwegen on 8 February 1945. In addition to the field, medium and heavy artillery of the Corps, a 'Pepperpot' was fired by a diverse collection of weapons: 4.2-inch mortars and Vickers machine guns of the infantry, 17-pounder anti-tank guns firing high explosive shells, 40mm Bofors guns of the Light Anti-Aircraft regiments and 75mm guns of Sherman tanks were all encouraged to thicken up the mixture and were allotted areas of the forward German defences as their targets. The artillery fire was estimated as varying between 650 and 1,300 shells per kilometre per hour, rising to a peak of 6,500 during the barrage, but the amount delivered by the Pepperpot was not amenable to calculation. The attack was a success, but it did not achieve success by any sudden demoralization of the defenders, merely by cutting communications and forcing the isolation of the units of the defence so that they could not be controlled effectively and thus could be defeated piecemeal.

Complete demoralization by artillery fire occurred now and then, but it is not possible to make dogmatic statements about rates of fire or weight of shell which will bring this about, as every case examined offers different conclusions. The most important factor seems to be the state of morale and discipline of the troops being bombarded. An example of this was to be seen in a small affair at Castel Del Rio in Italy in October 1944. A small German unit held a position in and around two isolated houses on a hill. These were engaged by two 25-pr guns which, firing an hour each in turn, shelled the position for five hours non-stop, sending a shell across every three minutes with clockwork regularity. Two hours later, after a further short bombardment by a regiment of 25-pounders, infantry advanced and took the position without opposition. Only two defenders were found alive; of the original force of about 60 men, 23 had been killed and 12 wounded, while the rest had 'withdrawn without orders' during the five-hour shelling. The psychological effect of one shell arriving regularly every three minutes had completely demoralized the garrison and, in the words of one of the survivors, had nearly driven them mad.

The Italian Campaign saw a large number of anti-aircraft guns diverted to the field role; this 3.7-inch was firing on the Gothic Line in August 1944, manned by 97 Battery, the London Scottish Regiment.

At the crossing of the Senio in North Italy by the New Zealand Division in April 1945 a barrage was fired which delivered 5,000lb of high explosive shells into every hundred square yards of the target area at a rate of about 40lb per minute. The post-battle report of 2 NZ Division noted that prisoners of war made statements 'testifying to the terrifying effect of the bombardment and to the low state of morale

beforehand.'

Invariably, it seems, where a complete collapse of the defence occurred, the defenders were second-class troops whose morale was poor; good troops can be neutralized and their defensive effort reduced, but they are rarely completely broken by artillery fire alone.

It is unfortunate that no comparable analysis was ever made of the effect of Russian artillery fire against the German Army, particularly in the latter stages of the war, since the Russian employment of artillery *en masse* beggars the imagination. The British strength for Operation 'Veritable' – the clearing of the Reichswald Forest – was 516 field, 280 medium, 122 heavy and 72 heavy anti-aircraft guns (firing in the ground role), aided by 188 machine guns, 80 4.2-inch mortars, 114 40mm light anti-aircraft guns, 60 tank guns, 24 17-pounder anti-tank guns and 12 32-barrel rocket-launchers, a total of 1,900 weapons. This was considered to be a formidable collection. Yet in January 1945, for the crossing of the Vistula, the Soviet Army massed 32,143 guns and mortars together with over 6,000 tanks and assault guns, and even if their command and control system was less flexible than that of the British or Americans, the effect of such an incredible mass of ordnance must have been devastating.

In the early days of the Russo-German struggle the Soviets were handicapped by the speed of the German advance and their own

Spanish 'Blue Division' troops taking over a battery of German 15cm howitzers before going into action on the Russian front.

defective organization, but they soon began to reassert their long-held faith in artillery, and the turning point might be considered to be the Stalingrad offensive. The Battle for Stalingrad has been well dissected over the past thirty years, so that there is little point in describing it in detail. Nevertheless the artillery aspect appears to have escaped most commentators and it is worth while bringing out the point that Stalingrad was, above all else, an artillery battle with infantry actions overlaid, and the reason for this lay in the German method of attack and the Russian method of defence.

The basic German system of attack was in three stages. First a reconnaisance by light tanks in the form of feint attacks designed to sound out the Russian defences and discover their anti-tank weapons. Secondly the 'Preparation by Fire', usually by air support dive-bombing the discovered positions and artillery bombarding the forward defensive elements. Finally came the main attack, usually on a limited front, either while the preparation by fire was in progress or immediately after it finished. The attack was spear-headed by armour, with accompanying infantry, their task being to occupy positions cleared by the tanks or to assist the tanks by dealing with anti-tank weapons.

The Soviets well appreciated that this sequence was to be expected in the Stalingrad action and they therefore planned their defence primarily as an anti-tank defence, the infantry's machine guns and riflemen being positioned so as to guard and protect the anti-tank guns. Moreover in the Soviet's book any gun capable of shooting at a tank was an anti-tank gun, and there were no sectarian divisions of responsibility based on calibre or unit title. The whole of the artillery, in one way or another, was directed against the German armour.

The method of achieving this was to arrange the artillery in 'belts' behind the battlefield. The first belt, immediately at the front, contained artillery positioned so as to be able to fire direct at approaching tanks. These guns were grouped in strongpoints, mutually supporting and protected by infantry weapons. In places which appeared to be particularly well suited to tank attack, troops of field guns designated as 'tank destroyers' were sited so as to swamp the lines of approach with fire. These tank destroyer troops were so firmly committed to their role that they were not included in the artillery command system and thus could not receive any orders or tasks involving indirect fire; tanks were their target, and nothing else.

Behind this forward zone was the 'zone of field artillery', in which the normal indirect-fire artillery was sited; behind this, the 'zone of medium artillery' and behind that the 'zone of heavy artillery'. Finally, at the rear, was a mobile reserve of all natures of guns and howitzers which could be used to reinforce a threatened area or as replacements for weapons damaged in the battle.

So far this is unexceptionable; but the Soviets now took their zoning

system and transferred it to the other side of the line. The German side of
the front was divided into similar zones into which the fire of a
particular zone of weapons would fall. Thus, from the line of contact (or
'front line') to the nearest skyline (usually one to two kilometres in the
area around Stalingrad) was reserved for the fire of the direct-shooting
weapons. The next zone, which corresponded to the zone of field
artillery on the Soviet side, was reserved as the target area for the field
artillery. Similarly zones of target areas for medium and heavy artillery
were delineated corresponding to the disposition of the guns on the
ground.

A Soviet 122mm
howitzer being
loaded.

With the zoning established fire plans were made to cover any
foreseeable pattern of attack, and the principle was laid down that the
three classes of artillery were to open fire on their own zones, beginning
with the rearmost. Thus, when an attack began to develop, the heavy
artillery opened the defence by bombarding planned targets in the
rearmost zone of their target area. As (and if) the attack persisted and
moved forward into the next zone, so the medium guns would begin
firing into their area of influence and, in turn, the field artillery would
open fire as the attack came closer.

Eventually, as the attack entered the final zone, the direct fire weapons would pick their targets and engage them. From this it can be seen that the strength of the defensive fire increased as the attack came closer to the Soviet position; also, that the initial stages of the attack, when the German armour would be reconnoitring to try and discover the Soviet forward defences, only the rear zones of Soviet guns would engage, and the forward guns would not reveal their positions.

Like all such schemes, of course, once the forward German elements actually got among the forward Soviet elements, the theories and suppositions went awry and the German advance was rarely stopped in its tracks quite as completely as the planned system hoped. Individual tanks or sections of tanks might break through the anti-tank screen, and in these cases the Soviet doctrine was to try and deal with them in detail and prevent these isolated elements coming together to form a nucleus for concerted action. Most of the textbooks would have called for counter-attacks in such circumstances, but the Soviets disagreed. Break-in was to be countered by the mobile reserve, rapidly throwing anti-tank guns into the path of the intruders and dealing with them piecemeal. If a counter-attack was necessary, due to a breakthrough by a powerful force, then it was mounted by Soviet tanks liberally supported by the mobile reserve of artillery, but this was only done as a last resort and was restricted to dealing with an immediate threat; there was no pushing

Another German 15cm howitzer, captured by Soviet troops in 1943.

The Proof of the Pudding

Soviet soldiers
examine a mixed
haul of German
guns. In the fore-
ground the 75mm
Infantry Gun 18
with its unique
'shotgun' breech; in
the rear, the 15cm
Infantry Gun 33.

A Soviet 76.2mm
anti-aircraft gun
carried on a motor
truck mounting.

Part of the massed artillery used in the Stalingrad counter-offensive.

A Soviet 76mm field gun M41 in an anti-tank position amid the ruins of a Stalingrad factory.

forward of the Soviet line, no attempt to carry the battle to the Germans. The defensive ring had been set up and the Germans could expend their energy in battering against it while the Soviets conserved theirs by simply maintaining the status quo.

An interesting point which arises from study of the battle is the virtual interchangeability of artillery equipments under the Soviet system. As was inevitable in such a bitterly-fought contest, the direct-fire guns in the forward zone suffered enormously, and they were replaced quite simply by whatever guns happened to be available for use. An anti-tank gun casualty might be replaced with a field gun, a howitzer with an anti-tank gun; if it could shoot, it went, and there was no distinction of type or role.

In the indirect fire zones maximum use was made of dispersion and camouflage to protect the guns from air attack, plus a high proportion of anti-aircraft artillery (most of which was so sited as to have a secondary anti-tank role if the need arose), while the tight perimeter allowed excellent communications, so that fire could be massed and moved about to deal with any threat.

Eventually the system took its toll, the armoured threat diminished and the tide turned. After the house-to-house fighting with which Stalingrad is most associated it became the turn of the Soviets to attack, producing the encirclement which sealed the fate of the German Sixth Army. When this attack was mounted it was supported by almost 7,000 guns and heavy mortars, many of which had been brought up to the east bank of the River Don for the purpose and which were, from all reports, literally crammed together wheel to wheel. With this huge array a barrage was fired which, according to eyewitnesses, turned the snow-covered ground into a black landscape of shell craters as far as the eye could see. It was a portent of the incredible masses of artillery which the Soviets were to employ in their advance on Berlin.

To accompany the use of massed artillery it became vital to improve the ability of the guns to find targets. In ancient days the guns fired at what they saw; during the First World War the matter of locating targets became more involved, but on a static front it was only a matter of time before the enemy dispositions became known and could be attacked. But in a modern war of movement, a war in which the enemy's defences could run to several miles in depth, the unaided human eye of an observer on the ground was incapable of detecting more than a small proportion of the possible targets.

The First World War saw the birth of a number of target location methods; manned and tethered observation balloons raised the eye-level of the observer and gave him a deeper reach across the lines, though at considerable risk, since the balloon was a favourite target for aviators – not for nothing were the balloon observers the only aeronauts to be provided with parachutes.

On the other side of the Stalingrad front a German 5cm PAK 38 anti-tank gun in a somewhat exposed position.

In order to detect enemy guns and mark them down for retaliatory fire, advantage was taken of the two physical characteristics of the gun, the flash of the propellant and the noise of discharge. Squads of observers were distributed across the front and provided with optical instruments, essentially powerful binoculars on a rotating graduated base. Working in concert these observers would observe the flash of a gun firing, turn their instruments on it, and by cross-observation and plotting on a map, arrive at the position of the gun. The sound of the gun's discharge could be detected by frequency-sensitive microphones buried in the ground; as these received the sound, so a signal passed down a wire to operate a pen on a recording instrument. With five or six microphones connected to one recorder the time interval between the sound's appearance at the different points could be analysed and the results used to determine the location of the enemy gun.

Finally the infant Royal Air Force was used to provide aerial observation and correction of fire, communicating with the guns by a variety of signal systems, most of which were notable for the facility with which the pilot could talk to the guns and the near-impossibility of the guns ever managing to deliver any sort of information or comment to the pilot.

After the war the flash-spotting and sound-ranging techniques were retained, the observation balloon was abandoned, and, as we have observed, the prospect of Air-Ground control of fire was viewed with some pessimism. In the 1920s and 1930s the Royal Artillery contained a number of officers who took up flying as a recreational activity, and these officers soon appreciated the value of a light aircraft to replace the observation balloon as an elevated viewpoint for the observation of fire. Brigadier Parham, already mentioned in connection with the development of fire control methods, was prominent among this group; in 1934 he qualified as an autogyro pilot, which was remarkable enough, and then bought a light aircraft and, in his own words, 'flew it until the engine fell out', after which he turned it into a glider and continued flying. Parham and his fellow aviators urged the formation of a light aircraft facility for the artillery, but the suggestion was bitterly resisted by the RAF, who were determined to retain control of anything which flew.

Eventually, in spite of much argument and resistance – in other quarters beside the RAF, it might be said – an experimental flight of Taylorcraft machines were sent to France in 1940, but the rapid advance of the Germans placed them at hazard and they were withdrawn to England without having flown operationally. But in 1941 it was finally admitted that the RAF had sufficient on their hands and could not take on the task of observing for the gunners. Air Observation Post (AOP) flights were formed and were first used in support of the British First Army in North Africa in 1942; as luck would have it, the Commander,

The Auster Air OP which, flying above the front, extends the artillery's command of the battle for several miles and permits the detection and engagement of targets which would not be seen from the normal ground-level observation posts.

The British Field Artillery Radar No. 1, a modified coast-watching set mounted on a half-track which appeared in the closing days of the war.

Royal Artillery, of this Army was none other than Parham, so that the flyers were assured of a sympathetic backing whatever happened. In the event, the AOPs proved that their contentions had been perfectly correct; they could survive in the face of enemy aircraft by flying low and using the terrain; they could control gunfire and pilot an aircraft at the same time; they could communicate vital information on enemy movement over and above their prime task of controlling the guns. From then on the AOP was an accepted part of the artillery scene and its employment increased.

The arrival of radar led a number of gunners to query its possible application as an instrument for detecting targets and directing guns, but in general there was never sufficient research and manufacturing potential to allow such a luxury as a field artillery radar set to be developed. The technique of radar was in its infancy too, and the many problems of target discrimination and ground interference were formidable. Coast artillery were given a few sets by way of experiment, the principal installations being in the Dover area, but the only applications in the field artillery sphere were a matter of private enterprise. Possibly because of their more liberal scale of equipment, the U.S. Army appear to have been the only people to have done much in this line. The U.S. XV Corps brought an SCR–584 Radar – nominally

an anti-aircraft search radar – into ground use in October 1944 to '. . .
provide battlefield intelligence, locate moving ground targets for Corps
artillery and to adjust friendly artillery fire . . .' with remarkable results:
'In the Gros-Rederching area the radar picked up what appeared to be a
considerable tank concentration moving down the road towards 44
Infantry Division. This target was plastered by both Div and Corps
artillery. PW later stated that this was a movement of tanks in
preparation for a counter-attack but that the artillery fire had been so
destructive the plan had to be cancelled.'

In all, 989 fire missions in the ground role were radar controlled in XV
Corps, a high percentage for that time and stage in radar development.

    The fact that XV Corps were able to 'borrow' an anti-aircraft radar
and put it to other use is indicative of two things: first that the
manufacture of sets had reached a satisfactory level, and secondly that
the requirement for air defence on the Allied side had diminished
considerably, due to Allied air superiority. On the other side of the fence
it was very different; not even was there no sign of radar being used for
directing ground fire, there was by no means sufficient radar for the anti-
aircraft defences. The German scientists had made the same
fundamental discoveries at much the same time as their British and
American counterparts, and by 1938 they had gun-directing radar sets on
ships of the German Navy. But two things conspired against them; in
the first place a radar reconnaisance by a detector-equipped Zeppelin off
the coast of Britain in 1938 failed to detect any evidence of radar activity –
largely because, as it later transpired, the Germans were seeking signals
in a frequency band not being used by British sets – and secondly the ill-
judged 'one year ban' previously mentioned, which cut the ground from
beneath most of the basic research without which electronic
development was impossible.

    But even with radar absent or, at best, in short supply, the German AA
defences were a well-organized, voluminous and highly effective force.
In 1939 the Luftwaffe Flak defences of Germany contained 6,500 light
and 2,450 medium guns. In June 1944, the time of their maximum
strength, the total was 30,463 light and 15,087 medium and heavy guns.
And a measure of their assessment of the threat is indicated by the
placing of the guns; 33,345 guns, including a major part of the heavy
and medium strength, were allotted to the western defences of Germany
to deal with British and American attacks, only 27 per cent of the
strength being deployed against the Soviets.

    The deployment of German flak in 1939 was in accordance with
peacetime policies which assumed that only daylight raids would take
place. Generally the effect of gunfire was considerably over-estimated
and a strength of 2½ 'Abteilungen' was considered sufficient to protect a
large town. An Abteilung contained three medium batteries (24 guns)
and two light batteries (24 guns). The basic defence was the

German 12.8cm
anti-aircraft gun,
their heaviest service
model, which fired a
55lb shell to a 35,000
foot effective ceiling.

Luftverteidigungszone West (LVZ West), formed shortly before the war
and consisting of heavy, medium and light flak deployed in a belt 30
kilometres deep stretching from the Black Forest to the Saar. This zone
was later extended, first to Aachen, then to the Heligoland Bight and
finally into Schleswig Holstein, to form a first line barrier.

In addition individual gun defended areas were established around likely targets. These were sited on the assumption that the bombers would fly at 250km/hr and 4,000 metres altitude, giving a bomb release line some 2,500 metres from the target. Guns were then sited so as to allow a 30-second engagement time before the attacking aircraft reached the bomb release line.

With the beginning of the first night raids on Germany it was found that the system of defence was too scattered and thin on the ground to produce good results. The first reaction was to concentrate more guns in the threatened areas, such as the Ruhr and Berlin, but eventually, in 1943, the formation of 'Grossbatterien' was authorized. This was a combination of gun troops and batteries to form a large battery of 18 88mm or 12 105mm or 128mm guns; these were sited on fresh assumptions of bomber performance – a speed of 425km/hr, altitude 8,000 metres, and a bomb release line 6 kilometres from the target. The 'Grossbatterie' was controlled by a single radar set feeding information to a predictor serving each troop of guns; in theory, two radars were supposed to be provided, one controlling an engagement while the other searched for the next target, but in practice the shortage of radar sets

The famous '88' was not the only German anti-aircraft gun to be used in ground action; this is the quadruple 20mm light AA gun firing in support of an infantry action on the Russian front in 1942.

prevented this. Indeed, one of the virtues of the system was that it saved on radar and technical personnel.

In addition to the Grossbatterien, 'Vorfeldbatterien' or 'Line of approach batteries' were deployed in suitable locations, and the resulting combination produced an increase in the concentration of fire which began to take its toll of Allied aircraft. At about this time the U.S. Air Force began daylight raiding, in tight formations at great altitude, and this in turn led to even greater concentrations of Grossbatterien, until some important targets were ringed with as many as 600 guns; some less important targets, of course, found themselves without any guns at all, their defences having been siphoned off to boost the gun strength of the more important areas.

The results of this concentration can be seen in the 8th U.S. Air Force returns for bombers destroyed or damaged by flak fire over Germany:

Period	Damaged	Destroyed
May-Aug 1943	1,594	88
Sep-Dec 1943	2,670	135
Jan-Feb 1944	2,878	98
Mar-Apr 1944	5,969	281
May-Jun 1944	7,920	286

It is noteworthy that at the end of the period shown above, flak was doing far more damage than were fighter aircraft. Flak downed 286, fighters 239; flak damaged 7,920, fighters 269. The Germans appreciated this difference as well; a postwar interrogation of a senior Flak officer contains the sentence 'There was a high regard for the effectiveness of Flak artillery as compared to that of fighter aircraft.'

An example of the practical application of these theories can be seen in the defence of Munich. At the end of 1941 the area was ringed by 6 light, 12 medium and 11 heavy batteries, a total of 75 20mm guns, 24 37mm guns and 66 88mm guns, together with about 45 searchlights. One radar was provided for each three heavy batteries; this was located near the centre of the batteries and data was passed to the guns by telephone, the batteries being responsible for converting the radar information into data applicable to their own locations.

In 1942 more radar sets became available until each battery was provided and, in addition, a number of 'Freya' long range early-warning sets appeared. In the middle of 1942, with the threat of heavier Allied raids, twelve more 88mm batteries, two 20mm batteries and ten batteries of searchlights were added, together with two batteries of 105mm guns, while the ring of guns, originally sited about 6 km from the city centre, was moved out to 8 km distance.

The first major raid on Munich was by the RAF on the night of 19/20 September 1942 and further raids occurred during the following winter. In the spring of 1943 the first Grossbatterien were formed by moving more units into the area, and in 1944 the continuing raids led to Munich being upgraded in importance to a Flak Divisional Command, the number of medium and heavy batteries being increased to 50. Munich was one of the areas involved in the experimental use of percussion-fuzed ammunition in the spring of 1945, and according to an interrogation of the Operations Officer of the Munich Defences it gave a 100 per cent increase in the effectiveness of fire. With time-fuzed shells 4,000 rounds per plane were needed; with percussion fuzed shells 2,000 rounds per plane became the average figure. Unfortunately he was unable to substantiate his opinion with reliable figures, and Allied Flak Intelligence staffs regarded them with scepticism largely because the time fuze figure seemed to be a remarkably poor one under the circumstances. Postwar analysis of the U.S. 1st Army AA gun firings, for example, showed a figure of 364 time-fuzed rounds for each aircraft downed and 233 proximity-fuzed rounds, figures so different as to throw considerable doubt on the Munich officer's claims.

In contrast to this, a highly specialized Allied anti-aircraft defensive system is of interest. The story of the defeat of the flying bomb attacks on London by fighters and artillery is fairly well known; less well known, though no less vital, was the defence of Antwerp against the same weapon.

'Antwerp X' was the code name for the gun defence of Antwerp and it remained secret and unknown until well after the war was over. In September 1944 Allied intelligence determined that the German Army would begin attacking Antwerp in late October with V-1 flying bombs – indeed, their information was so good that they forecast the first bomb to within 24 hours of its actual time of arrival. The reason behind the attack was to deny the port facilities to the Allies who needed them to supply the troops on the German borders, rather than having to rely on the long road supply line back to Normandy. Antwerp fell into Allied hands on 4 September 1944 and the Germans immediately began preparing launch sites for the missiles.

The British 80th AA Brigade, commanded by Brigadier Deacon, and comprising one light (40mm) and two heavy (3.7-inch) regiments began the Antwerp X defence in October, and on 23 October the U.S. 30th AAA Group, commanded by Col. R. W. Russell, moved in with 90mm guns, SCR584 radars and M9 electronic data computers. Proximity fuzes were provided for all guns except the 40mm, and at 0430 on 27 October 1944 the first V-1 appeared. It was promptly shot down by a 90mm gun of D Battery 126th AAA Gun Battalion U.S. Army; the second bomb appeared in the wake of the first at 0433 and met the same fate. From then until 30 March 1945 the Antwerp X defence was operative.

It is generally believed that V-1s were sitting ducks for gunners since they flew at a regular speed on a straight and level track. To some extent this was true, although the particular combination of speed and altitude

Antwerp defences
against the flying-
bomb; showing the
primary missile
tracks and the dis-
position of units.

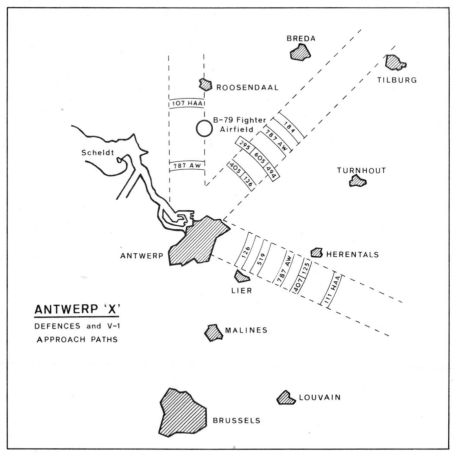

was a difficult one for the guns to cope with. But statistics proved that
the V-1 was, in fact, eight times more difficult to destroy than a
conventional aircraft flying at the same speed and height, because of the
small size, extremely robust construction, and lack of vulnerable components such as pilot, engines, delicate instruments, large fuel tanks
and so forth. Nevertheless the guns hammered them unmercifully. In
efforts to outwit the defences the launch sites were frequently changed so
as to bring the missiles in on a completely different course, but every
such shift was foreseen and forestalled by adding fresh gun batteries to
cover the lines of approach. The pressure was relentless; on the night of
15/16 February 1945 for example, no less than 160 missiles were
launched at Antwerp and the heavy guns of the defences fired over 15,000
rounds. Some American 90mm guns wore out three or four barrels in the
five months' action, while components such as breech blocks, believed
to be virtually everlasting, were beginning to show signs of wear.

When the battle ended and the arithmetic was done, the result was a
triumph for the gunners. Of the 4,883 bombs launched against Antwerp
only 156 managed to get through the ring of defensive guns; the port
never stopped work and millions of tons of stores were safely unloaded.

The 'kill' percentage was 97 per cent; and it must be stressed that the defence of Antwerp was, unlike the defence of Britain against the same threat, entirely an artillery defence. No fighter aircraft or balloons were used.

As the Allied air forces gained superiority the numbers of field army anti-aircraft guns became excessive for the relatively small number of air attacks they had to deal with. The amount of manpower locked up in these units and serving little useful purpose was considerable, and there was often pressure to disband anti-aircraft regiments and use the men in some other, more immediately vital, role. Sometimes this was done, and AA gunners found themselves retraining on field guns, mortars, anti-tank guns or rocket launchers, or even transmuted into infantry. But generally this sort of irreversible change was resisted by theatre commanders; perhaps the Allied side did have local air superiority today, but who knew what the enemy might have up his sleeve for tomorrow? A better system was to leave the AA gunners with their guns but persuade them to try something new, use the guns as field pieces against ground targets. They needed little persuasion, since anthing was preferable to scanning a blank sky day after day, and 'AA in the Ground

Another 3.7-inch in the ground role in Italy; the expression of the man at the right is indicative of the blast of these high-velocity guns when fired at low angles.

Role' became an extremely useful adjunct to the Division or Corps artillery.

There were, of course, a few technical problems to be solved first, but since the Vertical Gunners thrived on technical problems, these were rapidly overcome. Sights had to be fitted to allow terrestrial fire on the same principles as field artillery, siting and concealing such large guns brought its own problems, but the greatest difficulty lay in adapting the peculiar ballistics of AA guns to this sort of shooting. AA guns were equipped with fixed rounds of ammunition, with non-adjustable charges giving high velocities, and the high explosive shells were fitted with time fuzes. This meant that the trajectory was flat, the time of flight short, and the shells would only burst in the air and not on impact. The latter was soon resolved by the issue of percussion fuzes to replace the time models, but the former characteristics set observers some pretty problems. Due to the flat trajectory the inter-relation of gun and target had to be fairly precisely arranged so that the shell did not meet any terrain features or other obstructions in its flight, and, in addition, the flat trajectory allied with the usual laws of probability and distribution meant an extremely long 'zone' into which the shells were liable to fall plus and minus of the target. Once observers learned the quirks of the flat trajectory guns, good shooting could be done, but a field gun practitioner attempting to range an AA gun for the first time was almost guaranteed a minor apoplectic fit before he mastered the new technique.

An American 90mm Gun M1 deployed for anti-tank defence in Belgium in 1944.

But the drawbacks were small compared to the advantages; the

average medium AA gun had a ground range in excess of the comparable calibres of field guns – 20,600 yards for the British 3.7-inch, 19,000 yards for the U.S. 90mm gun; the AA gun fired at high velocity so that the shell arrived at the target before the sound of the gun's discharge, a psychological discomfort which was a great morale reducer; and the rate of fire of AA guns, upwards of 20 rounds a minute with pre-set or percussion fuzes, meant an overwhelming volume of fire on the target in a short space of time.

In Germany the U.S. Army frequently deployed 90mm AA guns as anti-tank weapons, and did great execution with them, and it was one of these which produced one of the most remarkable feats of gunnery of the entire war; a case of 'AA in the Ground Role in the AA Role.'

In December 1944, when the German Army made their desperate thrust at the Ardennes, the U.S. 110th AAA Gun Battalion was hurriedly withdrawn from its AA task and sent out to become an anti-tank screen in the Stavelot-Malmédy area. It must be stressed that all the anti-aircraft fire control equipment was left behind; the guns mounted direct-fire telescope sights only. On New Year's Day 1945 the German Air Force made an unexpected appearance in the combat area; after two or three Messerschmitt Me109s had flown low over his area, Staff-Sergeant F. J. Lucid, a gun commander, decided to try and do something about this. The next Me109 appeared, crossing his front, and Lucid's gunlayers tracked it with the anti-tank sight, 'aiming off' as if it were a tank. Lucid guessed at a fuze length of two seconds and set a time fuze accordingly;

Another '90' in action, this time on Bougainville against the Japanese ground forces. The gunner in the foreground holds the round in the mechanical fuze setter so as to set the time fuze for airburst fire.

the gun was loaded and, as the aircraft reached the crossing point, the shortest range between it and the gun, the round was fired. The shell burst just in front of the Messerschmitt; it began to emit smoke, turned back towards the German lines, lost height and crashed.

This incredible record of one shot, one plane, fired without benefit of any form of anti-aircraft fire control or sight, was testified to by numerous observers in the area and the gun was officially credited with the aircraft. One is inclined to feel sorry for the unfortunate pilot; the odds against such a thing happening to him must have been astronomical.

A sector of the artillery which tends to get forgotten is the coast defence branch, now long since disbanded by the major powers. Actual coast defence actions were few and far between during the war, being confined to Norway, Malta, Leghorn (a British battery beat off a German E-boat attack here in April 1944) and – though no details are known – probable actions at Sebastopol and Kronstadt by Soviet defences against German naval attacks. More notoriety attached to the non-coast defence actions of coast fortresses such as Singapore, Hong Kong and Manila Bay, disasters which it would be unjust to attribute to faults in the coast

The Soviets also used their anti-aircraft guns as anti-tank weapons when the need arose; this 85mm appears to be expecting visitors.

defence systems there. The coast guns did what they were intended to do – deter war vessels from coming into their zone of fire. The arrival of land forces from the other direction was not the sort of attack that the coast guns were sited to deal with, though in every case the guns did, where the terrain allowed it, turn and fire on the attackers. To be sure, anyone who had heard of Port Arthur ought not to have been surprised at the Japanese methods, and it is a dismal story of poverty and obstructionism which lies behind the failure of the defences in Singapore and Hong Kong. The American defences at Manila were a different matter, since they simply guarded the entrance to Manila Bay and their deterrent effect on a landing anywhere else in the Philippine Islands was obviously nil. Consequently the Japanese, very properly, left the Manila Bay forts alone until the rest of the Philippines had been taken, after which they simply instituted a siege; and since the forts were all on islands, the combination of bombardment and starvation led to their eventual surrender.

The Manila Bay defences were probably the most powerful group of coast forts in the world. Fort Mills (better known by the name of the island it encompassed, Corregidor), Fort Hughes, Fort Frank, and the 'Concrete Battleship' Fort Drum, disposed between them 8 14-inch guns, 24 12-inch howitzers, 8 12-inch guns, 11 6-inch guns, 14 3-pounders, 8 155mm guns, and 18 3-inch AA guns. By way of comparison, Singapore Fortress had 5 15-inch, 6 9.2-inch, 18 6-inch, 7 12-pounder and 10 6-pounder, while Hong Kong had 8 9.2-inch, 14 6-inch, 4 4-inch and 2 4.7-inch. The other noteworthy feature of the Manila Bay fortress was that the armament in 1941, except the AA guns,

An American 12-inch seacoast mortar is loaded. Mortars of this type, though obsolescent, were used to good effect against the Japanese Army on the Bataan peninsula in 1942.

The mortar battery fires, and a shell can be seen in flight. By siting four mortars together and firing them simultaneously the chances of striking a warship were much improved.

Fort Mills, the island of Corregidor, one of the most powerful concentrations of armament ever seen in a coast fortress.

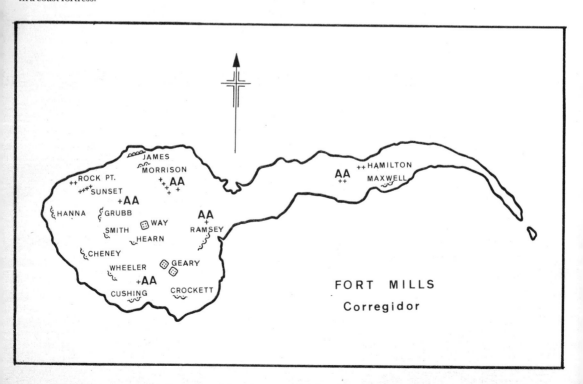

FORT MILLS
Corregidor

was that which had been installed before the First World War; the Washington Conference of 1922 and its clauses regarding fortification in the Pacific Area had been scrupulously (if naively) observed by Britain and the U.S.A., though Britain did manage to install a few guns in Hong Kong after 1939 and before the Japanese invasion. In Manila Bay, however, the only modernization had been a matter of exchanging two 12-inch gun mountings for more modern versions and the last-minute installation of three batteries of 155mm field guns on prepared emplacements.

It is of interest to compare the Japanese coast defences; in their case the effect of the Washington Conference was the opposite. While the fortification clause forbade strengthening defences, the Naval clauses limited vessels and armaments, and the Japanese Navy found itself with a number of battleship turrets mounting 41cm, 30cm and 25cm guns surplus to their needs. These were offered to the army, who gladly accepted them and, beginning in about 1926, installed these turrets in the fortresses guarding Tokyo Bay, the Shimonoseki Strait (between Japan and Korea) and the Tsugaru Strait (between Honshu and Hokkaido). These installations were, by any standards, lavish; the turrets were emplaced above extensive underground works containing magazines, engine rooms, accommodation and fire control. Air conditioning, gas-proofing and local defence were carefully attended to, and the fire control system was an electrical computing system well in advance of that used by any other nation at the time. However, as is the way of these things, none of these turrets ever fired in anger and they

Battery Pennsylvania, on the island of Oahu, built in 1943-45 from a naval triple 14-inch turret salvaged from the USS *Arizona* which had been sunk in the Pearl Harbour attack. Two turrets were salvaged and planned for installation as coast defence but only this one was completed.

were eventually demolished by the U.S. Occupation forces in 1945-46; the subterranean emplacements still exist though, and I am indebted to Cdr. D. P. Kirchner, U.S. Navy, for sending me plans and information on these installations.

A contrast to these meticulously-prepared but unused defences is the story of extemporization and furious activity presented by the defences of Dover during the war. In truth, Dover was a special case, since the majority of the armament installed there was for offensive rather than defensive use, to attack vessels passing through the Straits of Dover and to reply to the fire of German long range guns on the French coast. There is some discrepancy in the available records of the armament of Dover in 1939, but it seems likely that the serviceable guns totalled 6 9.2-inch, 6 6-inch, 5 12-pounders and 2 6-pounders. In the normal course of events this would have been more than enough, since Dover was, apart from its cross-Channel connections, not particularly important; indeed, most of the existing works were echoes from pre-1919 days when Dover had been a Naval base and thus merited more protection than it would have done as a commercial port.

Construction of the emplacement for Hougham Battery of 8-inch guns near Dover, in 1941. As such things go it was a simple installation, but this picture shows why coast defences could not appear overnight.

With the fall of France in 1940 the Germans began the installation of heavy guns on the French coast, supplementing them with railway guns, and, as part of the preamble to Operation 'Sealion', the projected invasion of England, set about denying the Straits to any non-Axis shipping and, for good measure, shelling Dover and other areas of Kent. The first steps at retaliation were taken in June 1940 when the Admiralty conferred with Vickers-Armstrong and authorized the installation of two 14-inch Naval guns in the Dover area, to be manned by Royal

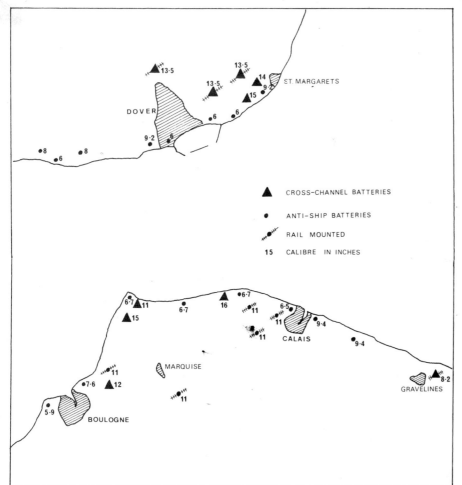

The cross-channel dispositions of British and German coast artillery. The positions marked with a triangle were capable of engaging land targets on the other side; the remainder were for the bombardment of shipping in the Channel.

Marines. These could fire a 1,586lb shell to almost 50,000 yards, and they were installed on modified naval barbette mounts. Mr Winston Churchill visited the first gun on 3rd August, which led to the Marines christening it 'Winnie'; by an obvious process, the second gun became 'Pooh'.

Meanwhile, in July, three elderly 13.5-inch naval guns had been taken from store and work began on assembling them to three ex-military railway truck mountings which had been standing idle since their 14-inch guns were made obsolete and scrapped in 1926. The first of these arrived in the Dover area, to be manned by Royal Marines, on 20 September 1940. The second static 14-inch was operational by February 1941 and all the railway guns by May. A fourth railway gun, the Army 18-inch howitzer, was also deployed in the area, but this weapon had insufficient range for cross-channel bombardment and was solely an anti-invasion measure.

While the Royal Marines now manned a comprehensive array of

ordnance, these weapons were only of use for bombarding enemy guns in France; their fire control and sighting systems were not suited to engaging moving targets such as ships, and so they could not be considered as defensive weapons, nor could they help in closing the Channel. In order to deal with shipping more specialized equipment was needed, and in September 1940 work began on five new batteries. Two (Fan Bay and Lydden Spout) each mounted 3 6-inch guns; one (South Foreland) 4 9.2-inch; one (Wanstone) 2 15-inch of the same type used at Singapore; and one (Hougham) 3 naval 8-inch on modified naval barbette mountings. All used the most modern patterns of mounting to allow 45° elevation and achieve the maximum range possible – 25,000 yards with the 6-inch, 31,000 with the 9.2-inch, 42,000 with the 15-inch and 29,200 with the 8-inch. With this equipment and the latest fire control equipment, the Channel could be completely dominated by the Dover guns. In addition, radar sets were specially developed for coast watching and gun direction and were located along the Kent and Sussex coastline. The first of the new batteries, the 6-inch, were installed by February 1941, the last, the 15-inch, being operational in June 1942.

A German 28cm Schiffskanone L/50 in a reinforced concrete casemate on the French coast, a much more complex structure than that of Hougham Battery.

Unfortunately that was just too late, since the greatest opportunity for the Dover guns arose on 12 February 1942 when the *Scharnhorst* and *Gneisenau,* screened by six destroyers and ten E-boats, made their

famous dash up the Channel. So far as coast artillery was concerned, the affair was not quite the fiasco for which they have often since been blamed. It has, for example, been said that German electronic jamming completely blinded all British radar; in fact the coast watching radar near Hastings detected the two battleships at the astonishing (for a set of that type at that time) range of 67,000 yards (38 miles) at 1050 a.m.; at 1130 the Lydden Spout battery radar also detected the targets and tracked them, and at 1215 the South Foreland set acquired them. What prevented the guns from dealing with the German warships was an ill-judged system of priorities; the Straits were the preserve of the Royal Navy and the Royal Air Force, and so long as their various elements were attempting to attack, the guns had to stay silent. Eventually the guns were given permission to open fire, and at 1219 the 9.2s of South Foreland Battery spoke – firing at a target now going away from them at high speed. The first shots were fired at a range of 30,000 yards, and 34 rounds were fired before the targets passed out of range; three rounds scored hits, but this was not sufficient to halt the fleeing convoy. Had the 15-inch been available, the story might have been different.

But there; had the 6-pounder been available in 1940; had Bataan peninsula been fortified; had the Germans had sufficient tungsten carbide; had there been self-propelled guns in 1940; one can go on for ever. War, and preparation for war, is a delicate balance of options and courses and the soldiers have perforce to make do with what they can get and fight the battles the best way they can. When the war was over and the German generals were questioned as to their experiences and opinions, they had some salutory things to say about various aspects of Allied

No. 3 gun of South Foreland Battery, near St. Margaret's, Kent, in March 1942. Conspicuous as it is at short range, it would be practically invisible to a ship at sea and a virtually impossible target for the ship's guns.

military operations, but there was one unanimous observation: the Allied artillery was the most consistently professional arm, the one which did the most damage, the one which made itself most persistently felt. And had the tables been turned, interrogation of Allied commanders might well have produced a similar assessment of German artillery. Irrespective of nationality, artillerymen tend towards professionalism. Except for a few minor eccentricities, gunners are content to let others follow the tactical will-o'-the-wisps and get-rich-quick theories of warfare. They know; artillery, skilfully handled and resolutely served provides support whenever and wherever needed, for 365 days a year, rain or shine, and that is the basic canvas onto which the picture of battle is painted. When the Second World War ended the long-range rocket and the nuclear explosive were touted as the new Messiah. The gun was obsolete, the missile and the aircraft were about to inherit the earth. In the futuristic nuclear holocaust prophesied by some writers, this might be so, since most of the world's surface will have been atomized into a cloud of steam in short order. But, fortunately, the world appears to have more sense than the Cassandras thought – though still not enough for us to dispense with armament entirely – and now, thirty years after, there is a fresh generation of guns appearing for the 1970s and 1980s. Guns much the same as those of the war years, using smokeless propellant to fire spun shells with mechanical fuzes and filled with high explosive; improved in detail, perhaps, often with improvements which can be traced back to one of the wartime developments we have discussed; controlled by computers and automatic data processing and all of electronic's artful aids. But guns, nevertheless. Born 1326 and still going strong.

BIBLIOGRAPHY

S. BIDWELL, *Gunners at War*, Arms and Armour, London
BASIL COLLIER, *The Defence of the United Kingdom*, HMSO, London
GEN. W. DORNBERGER, *V-2*, Hurst & Blackett, London
I. V. HOGG, *Artillery*, Macdonald and Jane's, London
I. V. HOGG, *German Artillery of the Second World War*, Arms and Armour, London
ERIC LINKLATER, *The Campaign in Italy*, HMSO, London
K. MACKSEY, *Guderian: Panzer General*, Macdonald and Jane's, London
A. MOOREHEAD, *The Desert War*, Hamilton, London
OSRD, *Rockets, Guns and Targets*, Houghton, Mifflin, Boston
GEN. SIR FREDERICK PILE, *Ack-Ack*, London
SIR FRANCIS TUKER, *Approach to Battle*, Cassell, London
J. S. WEEKS, *Men against Tanks*, David and Charles, Newton Abbott
Journal of the Royal Artillery, RA Institution, London
Journal of the US Coast Artillery, US CAA, Washington, DC

PHOTOGRAPH CREDITS

INDEX